this Powered by
- Chlorine -
SWIM LOGBOOK
BELONGS TO:

START DATE:

poweredbychlorine.com

Powered By Chlorine
Swimming Logbook
By AlyT & Born To Swim

Written by AlyT
Copyright 2024 by Allison Tyson. All rights reserved.

First printing: April, 2024

Disclaimer
While we draw on our professional expertise and background in teaching learn to swim and swimming training, by purchasing and reading our products you acknowledge that we have produced this book for informational and educational purposes only. You alone are solely responsible and take full responsibility for your own wellbeing as well as the health, lives and well-being of your family and children in your care in and around water.

Stay in touch:
Born to Swim, P.O Box 6699, Cairns City, QLD 4870
SwimMechanics@yahoo.com
www.BornToSwim.com.au
www.PoweredByChlorine.com
Instagram @LearnToSwimTheAustralianWay
Etsy Store www.borntoswimglobal.etsy.com
Most titles available from Etsy, Amazon and all good online Book Retailers

Other titles by this Author:
Water Awareness Newborns
Water Awareness Babies
Water Awareness Toddlers
Learn to Swim the Australian Way Level 1 The Foundations
Learn to Swim the Australian Way Level 2 The Basics
Learn to Swim the Australian Way Level 3 Intermediate
Learn to Swim the Australian Way Level 4 Advanced
The Ultimate Pool Party Planner
Focus On Freestyle: Teaching Guide
Water Safety: Teaching Guide
Breaststroke Bootcamp: Teaching Guide
Butterfly Bootcamp: Teaching Guide
Backstroke Bootcamp: Teaching Guide
Learning To Float: Color Me In & Learn To Swim Activity Book
A Float For Every Stroke: Teaching Body Position
Visual Aids For Inclusive Aquatic Education: 100+ Swimming Flashcards
Welcome To Swim Squad: Activity Book For Swimmers
Eat Pray Swim: A Swimmer's Logbook & Prayer Journal
Thalassophile: Logbook & Journal For Lovers Of The Ocean and Sea
Wild Swimming Quotes Coloring Book For Adults : Activity Book For Open Water Swimmers
Powered By Chlorine : Logbooks & Journals For Swimmers

Powered by Chlorine
VISION BOARD

Powered by Chlorine
VISION BOARD

Powered by Chlorine
MONTHLY GOAL SETTING

This month I want to ...

This month I want to ...

This month I want to ...

This month I want to ...

This month I want to ...

This month I want to ...

Powered by Chlorine
MONTHLY GOAL SETTING

This month I want to ...

This month I want to ...

This month I want to ...

This month I want to ...

This month I want to ...

This month I want to ...

Powered by
Chlorine
SWIM LOGBOOK

Coach:

Time:

Location:

Date: /   /20

S M T W T F S

Pool:
25 ◯ 50 ◯ Other ◯

Weather:

Training Type:
Swim ◯ Dryland ◯ Other ◯

TRAINING SESSION
Nº of laps: ....   Distance Swum: ....

WARM-UP MAIN SET COOL-DOWN
INTERVALS SPRINTS DIVES STARTS TURNS
DRILLS PULL BUOY FINS OTHER

Mood Tracker
Pre-workout:
Post-workout:

Thoughts & Reflections

Did I get enough...
water   sleep
Y N   Y N

Meals	Today I ate:
• BREAKFAST	
• LUNCH	
• DINNER	
• SNACKS	

Total Time Spent In The Water: ....
Rate today's workout: /10

TRAINING ENERGY LEVELS
Before   After

Best part about today was ...

Feedback...

Today's Goal:

Powered by
Chlorine
SWIM LOGBOOK

Coach:

Time:

Location:

Date: / /20

S M T W T F S

Pool:
25 ◯ 50 ◯ Other ◯

Weather:

Training Type:
Swim ◯ Dryland ◯ Other ◯

TRAINING SESSION
Nº of laps: .... Distance Swum: ....

WARM-UP MAIN SET COOL-DOWN
INTERVALS SPRINTS DIVES STARTS TURNS
DRILLS PULL BUOY FINS OTHER

Mood Tracker
Pre-workout:
Post-workout:

Thoughts & Reflections

Did I get enough...
water   sleep
Y N   Y N

Meals	Today I ate:
• BREAKFAST	
• LUNCH	
• DINNER	
• SNACKS	

Total Time Spent In The Water: ....
Rate today's workout: /10

TRAINING ENERGY LEVELS
Before   After

Best part about today was ...

Feedback...

Today's Goal:

Powered by
Chlorine
SWIM LOGBOOK

Coach:

Location:

Pool:
25 ○   50 ○   Other ○

Time:

Date: /   /20

S M T W T F S

Weather: ☀️ ⛅ 🌧️ 🌧️ ❄️

Training Type:
Swim ○   Dryland ○   Other ○

TRAINING SESSION
Nº of laps: ....   Distance Swum: ....

WARM-UP   MAIN SET   COOL-DOWN
INTERVALS   SPRINTS   DIVES   STARTS   TURNS
DRILLS   PULL BUOY   FINS   OTHER

Total Time Spent In The Water: ....
Rate today's workout: /10

Mood Tracker
Pre-workout: 😊 😃 😐 🤢 😣 😎
Post-workout: 😊 😃 😐 🤢 😣 😎

Thoughts & Reflections
_____
_____
_____
_____
_____
_____
_____

Did I get enough...
water   sleep
Y N   Y N

Meals	Today I ate:
• BREAKFAST	
• LUNCH	
• DINNER	
• SNACKS	

TRAINING ENERGY LEVELS
Before   After

Best part about today was ...

Feedback...

Today's Goal:

Powered by
Chlorine
SWIM LOGBOOK

Coach:

Location:

Time:

Date: / /20

S M T W T F S

Pool: 25 ○ 50 ○ Other ○

Training Type:
Swim ○ Dryland ○ Other ○

Weather:

TRAINING SESSION
Nº of laps: .... Distance Swum: ....

WARM-UP   MAIN SET   COOL-DOWN
INTERVALS   SPRINTS   DIVES   STARTS   TURNS
DRILLS   PULL BUOY   FINS   OTHER

Mood Tracker
Pre-workout:
Post-workout:

Thoughts & Reflections

Did I get enough...
water — Y N
sleep — Y N

Meals	Today I ate:
• BREAKFAST	
• LUNCH	
• DINNER	
• SNACKS	

Total Time Spent In The Water: ....
Rate today's workout: /10

TRAINING ENERGY LEVELS
Before   After

Best part about today was ...

Feedback...

Today's Goal:

Powered by
Chlorine
SWIM LOGBOOK

Coach:

Time:

Location:

Date: /   /20

S M T W T F S

Pool:
25 ◯ 50 ◯ Other ◯

Training Type:
Swim ◯ Dryland ◯ Other ◯

Weather:

TRAINING SESSION
Nº of laps: ....   Distance Swum: ....

WARM-UP   MAIN SET   COOL-DOWN
INTERVALS   SPRINTS   DIVES   STARTS   TURNS
DRILLS   PULL BUOY   FINS   OTHER

Mood Tracker
Pre-workout:
Post-workout:

Thoughts & Reflections

Did I get enough...
water   Y N
sleep   Y N

Meals	Today I ate:
• BREAKFAST	
• LUNCH	
• DINNER	
• SNACKS	

Total Time Spent In The Water: ....
Rate today's workout: /10

TRAINING ENERGY LEVELS
Before   After

Best part about today was ...

Feedback...

Today's Goal:

Powered by

Chlorine
SWIM LOGBOOK

Coach:

Location:

Pool: 25 ◯ 50 ◯ Other ◯

Time:

Date: / /20

S M T W T F S

Weather: ☀️ ⛅ 🌧️ ☁️ ❄️

Training Type:
Swim ◯ Dryland ◯ Other ◯

TRAINING SESSION
Nº of laps: .... Distance Swum: ....

WARM-UP MAIN SET COOL-DOWN
INTERVALS SPRINTS DIVES STARTS TURNS
DRILLS PULL BUOY FINS OTHER

Mood Tracker
Pre-workout: 😊 🥺 😐 🤪 😠 😎
Post-workout: 😊 🥺 😐 🤪 😠 😎

Thoughts & Reflections
....
....
....
....
....
....
....

Did I get enough...
water Y N   sleep Y N

Meals	Today I ate:
• BREAKFAST	
• LUNCH	
• DINNER	
• SNACKS	

Total Time Spent In The Water: ....
Rate today's workout: /10

TRAINING ENERGY LEVELS
Before   After

Best part about today was ...

Feedback...

Today's Goal:

Powered by
Chlorine
SWIM LOGBOOK

Coach:

Time:

Location:

Date: / /20

S M T W T F S

Pool:
25 ◯ 50 ◯ Other ◯

Training Type:
Swim ◯ Dryland ◯ Other ◯

Weather: ☀️ ⛅ 🌦️ ☁️ ❄️

TRAINING SESSION
Nº of laps: .... Distance Swum: ....

WARM-UP   MAIN SET   COOL-DOWN
INTERVALS SPRINTS DIVES STARTS TURNS
DRILLS   PULL BUOY   FINS   OTHER

Mood Tracker
Pre-workout: 🙂 😳 😐 😂 😠 😡 😎
Post-workout: 🙂 😳 😐 😂 😠 😡 😎

Thoughts & Reflections
_____
_____
_____
_____
_____
_____
_____

Did I get enough...
water Y N   sleep Y N

Meals	Today I ate:
• BREAKFAST	
• LUNCH	
• DINNER	
• SNACKS	

Total Time Spent In The Water: ....
Rate today's workout: /10

TRAINING ENERGY LEVELS
Before   After

Best part about today was ...

Feedback...

Today's Goal:

Powered by
Chlorine
SWIM LOGBOOK

Coach:

Location:

Time:

Date: /   /20

S M T W T F S

Pool:
25 ◯ 50 ◯ Other ◯

Training Type:
Swim ◯ Dryland ◯ Other ◯

Weather:

TRAINING SESSION
Nº of laps: ....   Distance Swum: ....

WARM-UP   MAIN SET   COOL-DOWN
INTERVALS   SPRINTS   DIVES   STARTS   TURNS
DRILLS   PULL BUOY   FINS   OTHER

Mood Tracker
Pre-workout:
Post-workout:

Thoughts & Reflections

Did I get enough...
water   Y N
sleep   Y N

Meals	Today I ate:
• BREAKFAST	
• LUNCH	
• DINNER	
• SNACKS	

Total Time Spent In The Water: ....
Rate today's workout: /10

TRAINING ENERGY LEVELS
Before   After

Best part about today was ...

Feedback...

Today's Goal:

Powered by
Chlorine
SWIM LOGBOOK

Coach:

Location:

Time:

Date: /   /20

S M T W T F S

Pool:
25 ◯ 50 ◯ Other ◯

Training Type:
Swim ◯ Dryland ◯ Other ◯

Weather:

TRAINING SESSION
Nº of laps: .... Distance Swum: ....

WARM-UP MAIN SET COOL-DOWN
INTERVALS SPRINTS DIVES STARTS TURNS
DRILLS PULL BUOY FINS OTHER

Mood Tracker
Pre-workout: 😊 😳 😐 🤪 😣 😎
Post-workout: 😊 😳 😐 🤪 😣 😎

Thoughts & Reflections

Did I get enough...
water   sleep
Y N   Y N

Meals	Today I ate:
• BREAKFAST	
• LUNCH	
• DINNER	
• SNACKS	

Total Time Spent In The Water: ....
Rate today's workout: /10

TRAINING ENERGY LEVELS
Before   After

Best part about today was ...

Feedback...

Today's Goal:

Powered by
Chlorine
SWIM LOGBOOK

Coach:

Location:

Pool: 25 ◯ 50 ◯ Other ◯

Time:

Date: / /20

S M T W T F S

Weather: ☀️ ⛅ 🌧️ 💧 ❄️

Training Type:
Swim ◯ Dryland ◯ Other ◯

TRAINING SESSION
Nº of laps: .... Distance Swum: ....

WARM-UP   MAIN SET   COOL-DOWN
INTERVALS   SPRINTS   DIVES   STARTS   TURNS
DRILLS   PULL BUOY   FINS   OTHER

Total Time Spent In The Water: ....
Rate today's workout: /10

Mood Tracker
Pre-workout: 😊 😳 😐 🥴 😠 😎
Post-workout: 😊 😳 😐 🥴 😠 😎

Thoughts & Reflections
....
....
....
....
....
....

Did I get enough...
water   sleep
Y N   Y N

Meals	Today I ate:
• BREAKFAST	
• LUNCH	
• DINNER	
• SNACKS	

TRAINING ENERGY LEVELS
Before   After

Best part about today was ...

Feedback...

Today's Goal:

Powered by
Chlorine
SWIM LOGBOOK

Coach:

Time:

Location:

Date: /   /20

S M T W T F S

Pool:
25 ◯   50 ◯   Other ◯

Weather:

Training Type:
Swim ◯ Dryland ◯ Other ◯

TRAINING SESSION
Nº of laps: ....   Distance Swum: ....

WARM-UP   MAIN SET   COOL-DOWN
INTERVALS   SPRINTS   DIVES   STARTS   TURNS
DRILLS   PULL BUOY   FINS   OTHER

Mood Tracker
Pre-workout: 😊 😬 😐 🤪 😠 😎
Post-workout: 😊 😬 😐 🤪 😠 😎

Thoughts & Reflections

_____
_____
_____
_____
_____
_____

Did I get enough...
water   sleep
Y N   Y N

Meals	Today I ate:
• BREAKFAST	
• LUNCH	
• DINNER	
• SNACKS	

Total Time Spent In The Water: ....
Rate today's workout: /10

TRAINING ENERGY LEVELS
Before   After

Best part about today was ...

Feedback...

Today's Goal:

Powered by
Chlorine
SWIM LOGBOOK

Coach:

Location:

Pool:
25 ◯ 50 ◯ Other ◯

Training Type:
Swim ◯ Dryland ◯ Other ◯

Time:

Date: / /20

S M T W T F S

Weather: ☀ ☁ 🌧 🌦 ❄

TRAINING SESSION
Nº of laps: .... Distance Swum: ....

WARM-UP MAIN SET COOL-DOWN
INTERVALS SPRINTS DIVES STARTS TURNS
DRILLS PULL BUOY FINS OTHER

Total Time Spent In The Water: ....
Rate today's workout: /10

Mood Tracker
Pre-workout: 😊 😴 😐 🤪 😠 😎
Post-workout: 😊 😴 😐 🤪 😠 😎

Thoughts & Reflections

Did I get enough...
water   sleep
Y N   Y N

Meals	Today I ate:
• BREAKFAST	
• LUNCH	
• DINNER	
• SNACKS	

TRAINING ENERGY LEVELS
Before   After

Best part about today was ...

Feedback...

Today's Goal:

Powered by
Chlorine
SWIM LOGBOOK

Coach:

Location:

Pool:
25 ◯ 50 ◯ Other ◯

Time:

Date: /   /20

S M T W T F S

Weather: ☀️ ⛅ 🌦️ 🌧️ ❄️

Training Type:
Swim ◯ Dryland ◯ Other ◯

TRAINING SESSION
Nº of laps: ……………….   Distance Swum: …………

WARM-UP   MAIN SET   COOL-DOWN
INTERVALS   SPRINTS   DIVES   STARTS   TURNS
DRILLS   PULL BUOY   FINS   OTHER

Mood Tracker
Pre-workout: 😊 😵 😂 😠 😡 😎
Post-workout: 😊 😵 😂 😠 😡 😎

Thoughts & Reflections

....
....
....
....
....
....
....

Did I get enough…
water   sleep
Y N   Y N

Meals	Today I ate:
• BREAKFAST	
• LUNCH	
• DINNER	
• SNACKS	

Total Time Spent In The Water: ………………
Rate today's workout: /10

TRAINING ENERGY LEVELS
Before   After

Best part about today was …

Feedback…

Today's Goal:

Powered by Chlorine
SWIM LOGBOOK

Coach:

Location:

Time:

Date: / /20

S M T W T F S

Training Type:
Swim ○ Dryland ○ Other ○

Pool:
25 ○ 50 ○ Other ○

Weather:

TRAINING SESSION
Nº of laps: .... Distance Swum: ....

WARM-UP MAIN SET COOL-DOWN
INTERVALS SPRINTS DIVES STARTS TURNS
DRILLS PULL BUOY FINS OTHER

Total Time Spent In The Water: ....
Rate today's workout: /10

Mood Tracker
Pre-workout:
Post-workout:

Thoughts & Reflections

Did I get enough...
water Y N
sleep Y N

Meals	Today I ate:
• BREAKFAST	
• LUNCH	
• DINNER	
• SNACKS	

TRAINING ENERGY LEVELS
Before After

Best part about today was ...

Feedback...

Today's Goal:

Powered by
Chlorine
SWIM LOGBOOK

Coach:

Time:

Location:

Date: /   /20

S M T W T F S

Training Type:
Swim ○ Dryland ○ Other ○

Pool:
25 ○ 50 ○ Other ○

Weather:

TRAINING SESSION
Nº of laps: .... Distance Swum: ....

WARM-UP   MAIN SET   COOL-DOWN
INTERVALS   SPRINTS   DIVES   STARTS   TURNS
DRILLS   PULL BUOY   FINS   OTHER

Mood Tracker
Pre-workout:
Post-workout:

Thoughts & Reflections

Did I get enough...
water   sleep
Y N   Y N

Meals	Today I ate:
• BREAKFAST	
• LUNCH	
• DINNER	
• SNACKS	

Total Time Spent In The Water: ....
Rate today's workout: /10

TRAINING ENERGY LEVELS
Before   After

Best part about today was ...

Feedback...

Today's Goal:

Powered by
Chlorine
SWIM LOGBOOK

Coach:

Location:

Pool: 25 ◯ 50 ◯ Other ◯

Time:

Date: __ / __ /20

S M T W T F S

Weather:

Training Type:
Swim ◯ Dryland ◯ Other ◯

TRAINING SESSION
Nº of laps: .... Distance Swum: ....

WARM-UP MAIN SET COOL-DOWN
INTERVALS SPRINTS DIVES STARTS TURNS
DRILLS PULL BUOY FINS OTHER

Total Time Spent In The Water: ....
Rate today's workout: /10

Mood Tracker
Pre-workout: 😌😧😐🤪😣😎
Post-workout: 😌😧😐🤪😣😎

Thoughts & Reflections

Did I get enough...
water Y N
sleep Y N

Meals	Today I ate:
• BREAKFAST	
• LUNCH	
• DINNER	
• SNACKS	

TRAINING ENERGY LEVELS
Before After

Best part about today was ...

Feedback...

Today's Goal:

Powered by
Chlorine
SWIM LOGBOOK

Coach:

Time:

Location:

Date: / /20

S M T W T F S

Pool: 25 ○ 50 ○ Other ○

Weather:

Training Type: Swim ○ Dryland ○ Other ○

TRAINING SESSION
Nº of laps: .... Distance Swum: ....

WARM-UP MAIN SET COOL-DOWN
INTERVALS SPRINTS DIVES STARTS TURNS
DRILLS PULL BUOY FINS OTHER

Mood Tracker
Pre-workout:
Post-workout:

Thoughts & Reflections

Did I get enough...
water Y N   sleep Y N

Meals	Today I ate:
• BREAKFAST	
• LUNCH	
• DINNER	
• SNACKS	

Total Time Spent In The Water: ....
Rate today's workout: /10

TRAINING ENERGY LEVELS
Before   After

Best part about today was ...

Feedback...

Today's Goal:

Powered by
Chlorine
SWIM LOGBOOK

Coach:

Location:

Time:

Date: /   /20

S M T W T F S

Pool:
25 ◯ 50 ◯ Other ◯

Training Type:
Swim ◯ Dryland ◯ Other ◯

Weather:

TRAINING SESSION
Nº of laps: ....   Distance Swum: ....

WARM-UP   MAIN SET   COOL-DOWN
INTERVALS   SPRINTS   DIVES   STARTS   TURNS
DRILLS   PULL BUOY   FINS   OTHER

Total Time Spent In The Water: ....
Rate today's workout: /10

Mood Tracker
Pre-workout: 😊 😳 😐 🥴 😣 😎
Post-workout: 😊 😳 😐 🥴 😣 😎

Thoughts & Reflections

Did I get enough...
water   sleep
Y N   Y N

Meals	Today I ate:
• BREAKFAST	
• LUNCH	
• DINNER	
• SNACKS	

TRAINING ENERGY LEVELS
Before   After

Best part about today was ...

Feedback...

Today's Goal:

Powered by
Chlorine
SWIM LOGBOOK

Coach:

Location:

Pool:
25 ◯ 50 ◯ Other ◯

Time:

Date: / /20

S M T W T F S

Weather:

Training Type:
Swim ◯ Dryland ◯ Other ◯

TRAINING SESSION
Nº of laps: .... Distance Swum: ....

WARM-UP   MAIN SET   COOL-DOWN
INTERVALS SPRINTS DIVES STARTS TURNS
DRILLS PULL BUOY FINS OTHER

Mood Tracker
Pre-workout:
Post-workout:

Thoughts & Reflections

Did I get enough...
water   sleep
Y N   Y N

Meals	Today I ate:
• BREAKFAST	
• LUNCH	
• DINNER	
• SNACKS	

Total Time Spent In The Water: ....
Rate today's workout: /10

TRAINING ENERGY LEVELS
Before   After

Best part about today was ...

Feedback...

Today's Goal:

Powered by
Chlorine
SWIM LOGBOOK

Coach:

Time:

Location:

Date: ___ / ___ /20

S M T W T F S

Pool:
25 ◯ 50 ◯ Other ◯

Weather:

Training Type:
Swim ◯ Dryland ◯ Other ◯

TRAINING SESSION
Nº of laps: .... Distance Swum: ....

WARM-UP   MAIN SET   COOL-DOWN
INTERVALS   SPRINTS   DIVES   STARTS   TURNS
DRILLS   PULL BUOY   FINS   OTHER

Mood Tracker
Pre-workout: 😊 🥵 😉 🤪 😣 😎
Post-workout: 😊 🥵 😉 🤪 😣 😎

Thoughts & Reflections
_____
_____
_____
_____
_____
_____
_____

Did I get enough...
water   sleep
Y N   Y N

Meals	Today I ate:
• BREAKFAST	
• LUNCH	
• DINNER	
• SNACKS	

Total Time Spent In The Water: ....
Rate today's workout: ___/10

TRAINING ENERGY LEVELS
Before   After

Best part about today was ...

Feedback...

Today's Goal:

Powered by
Chlorine
SWIM LOGBOOK

Coach:

Time:

Location:

Date: / /20

S M T W T F S

Pool:
25 ◯ 50 ◯ Other ◯

Training Type:
Swim ◯ Dryland ◯ Other ◯

Weather:

TRAINING SESSION
Nº of laps: .... Distance Swum: ....

WARM-UP   MAIN SET   COOL-DOWN
INTERVALS   SPRINTS   DIVES   STARTS   TURNS
DRILLS   PULL BUOY   FINS   OTHER

Mood Tracker
Pre-workout:
Post-workout:

Thoughts & Reflections

Did I get enough...
water   sleep
Y N   Y N

Meals	Today I ate:
• BREAKFAST	
• LUNCH	
• DINNER	
• SNACKS	

Total Time Spent In The Water: ....
Rate today's workout: /10

TRAINING ENERGY LEVELS
Before   After

Best part about today was ...

Feedback...

Today's Goal:

Powered by
Chlorine
SWIM **LOGBOOK**

Coach:

Location:

Pool:
25 ◯ 50 ◯ Other ◯

Training Type:
Swim ◯ Dryland ◯ Other ◯

Time:

Date: / /20

S M T W T F S

Weather: ☀ ⛅ 🌧 🌧 ❄

TRAINING SESSION
Nº of laps: .... Distance Swum: ....

WARM-UP MAIN SET COOL-DOWN
INTERVALS SPRINTS DIVES STARTS TURNS
DRILLS PULL BUOY FINS OTHER

Mood Tracker
Pre-workout: 😊 😳 😐 🤢 😖 😠 😎
Post-workout: 😊 😳 😐 🤢 😖 😠 😎

Thoughts & Reflections
_____
_____
_____
_____
_____
_____
_____

Did I get enough...
water 💤 sleep
Y N   Y N

Meals	Today I ate:
• BREAKFAST	
• LUNCH	
• DINNER	
• SNACKS	

Total Time Spent In The Water: ....
Rate today's workout: /10

TRAINING ENERGY LEVELS
Before   After

Best part about today was ...

Feedback...

Today's Goal:

Powered by Chlorine
SWIM LOGBOOK

Coach:

Time:

Location:

Date: / /20

S M T W T F S

Pool: 25 ◯ 50 ◯ Other ◯

Weather:

Training Type:
Swim ◯ Dryland ◯ Other ◯

TRAINING SESSION
Nº of laps: .... Distance Swum: ....

WARM-UP MAIN SET COOL-DOWN
INTERVALS SPRINTS DIVES STARTS TURNS
DRILLS PULL BUOY FINS OTHER

Mood Tracker
Pre-workout:
Post-workout:

Thoughts & Reflections

Did I get enough...
water Y N
sleep Y N

Meals	Today I ate:
• BREAKFAST	
• LUNCH	
• DINNER	
• SNACKS	

Total Time Spent In The Water: ....
Rate today's workout: /10

TRAINING ENERGY LEVELS
Before   After

Best part about today was ...

Feedback...

Today's Goal:

Powered by
Chlorine
SWIM LOGBOOK

Coach:

Time:

Location:

Date: / /20

S M T W T F S

Pool:
25 ○ 50 ○ Other ○

Training Type:
Swim ○ Dryland ○ Other ○

Weather:

TRAINING SESSION
Nº of laps: .... Distance Swum: ....

WARM-UP MAIN SET COOL-DOWN
INTERVALS SPRINTS DIVES STARTS TURNS
DRILLS PULL BUOY FINS OTHER

Mood Tracker
Pre-workout:
Post-workout:

Thoughts & Reflections

Did I get enough...
water   sleep
Y N   Y N

Meals	Today I ate:
• BREAKFAST	
• LUNCH	
• DINNER	
• SNACKS	

Total Time Spent In The Water: ....
Rate today's workout: /10

TRAINING ENERGY LEVELS
Before   After

Best part about today was ...

Feedback...

Today's Goal:

Powered by

Chlorine
SWIM LOGBOOK

Coach:

Time:

Location:

Date: / /20

S M T W T F S

Pool:
25 ◯ 50 ◯ Other ◯

Training Type:
Swim ◯ Dryland ◯ Other ◯

Weather:

TRAINING SESSION
Nº of laps: .... Distance Swum: ....

WARM-UP   MAIN SET   COOL-DOWN
INTERVALS SPRINTS DIVES STARTS TURNS
DRILLS PULL BUOY FINS OTHER

Mood Tracker
Pre-workout:
Post-workout:

Thoughts & Reflections

Did I get enough...
water   sleep
Y N   Y N

Meals	Today I ate:
• BREAKFAST	
• LUNCH	
• DINNER	
• SNACKS	

Total Time Spent In The Water: ....
Rate today's workout: /10

TRAINING ENERGY LEVELS
Before   After

Best part about today was ...

Feedback...

Today's Goal:

Powered by
Chlorine
SWIM LOGBOOK

Coach:

Location:

Pool:
25 ◯ 50 ◯ Other ◯

Training Type:
Swim ◯ Dryland ◯ Other ◯

Time:

Date: / /20

S M T W T F S

Weather:

TRAINING SESSION
Nº of laps: .... Distance Swum: ....

WARM-UP   MAIN SET   COOL-DOWN
INTERVALS   SPRINTS   DIVES   STARTS   TURNS
DRILLS   PULL BUOY   FINS   OTHER

Total Time Spent In The Water: ....
Rate today's workout: /10

Mood Tracker
Pre-workout: 😊 😣 😐 🤢 😠 😎
Post-workout: 😊 😣 😐 🤢 😠 😎

Thoughts & Reflections

Did I get enough...
water   sleep
Y N   Y N

Meals	Today I ate:
• BREAKFAST	
• LUNCH	
• DINNER	
• SNACKS	

TRAINING ENERGY LEVELS
Before   After

Best part about today was ...

Feedback...

Today's Goal:

Powered by
Chlorine
SWIM LOGBOOK

Coach:

Location:

Time:

Date: /   /20

S M T W T F S

Pool:
25 ◯ 50 ◯ Other ◯

Training Type:
Swim ◯ Dryland ◯ Other ◯

Weather:

TRAINING SESSION
Nº of laps: ....   Distance Swum: ....

WARM-UP   MAIN SET   COOL-DOWN
INTERVALS   SPRINTS   DIVES   STARTS   TURNS
DRILLS   PULL BUOY   FINS   OTHER

Mood Tracker
Pre-workout: 😊 😵 😐 😤 😠 😎
Post-workout: 😊 😢 😐 😤 😠 😩

Thoughts & Reflections

Did I get enough...
water   sleep
Y N   Y N

Meals	Today I ate:
• BREAKFAST	
• LUNCH	
• DINNER	
• SNACKS	

Total Time Spent In The Water: ....
Rate today's workout: /10

TRAINING ENERGY LEVELS
Before   After

Best part about today was ...

Feedback...

Today's Goal:

Powered by
Chlorine
SWIM LOGBOOK

Coach:

Location:

Pool:
25 ○ 50 ○ Other ○

Training Type:
Swim ○ Dryland ○ Other ○

Time:

Date: /   /20

S M T W T F S

Weather: ☀ ⛅ 🌦 🌧 ❄

TRAINING SESSION
Nº of laps: .... Distance Swum: ....

WARM-UP   MAIN SET   COOL-DOWN
INTERVALS SPRINTS DIVES STARTS TURNS
DRILLS   PULL BUOY   FINS   OTHER

Total Time Spent In The Water: ....
Rate today's workout: /10

Mood Tracker
Pre-workout: 😊 😳 😕 🤢 😣 😠 😎
Post-workout: 😊 😳 😕 🤢 😣 😠 😎

Thoughts & Reflections

Did I get enough...
water   sleep
Y N   Y N

Meals	Today I ate:
• BREAKFAST	
• LUNCH	
• DINNER	
• SNACKS	

TRAINING ENERGY LEVELS
Before   After

Best part about today was ...

Feedback...

Today's Goal:

Powered by Chlorine
SWIM LOGBOOK

Coach:

Time:

Location:

Date: / /20

S M T W T F S

Pool: 25 ◯ 50 ◯ Other ◯

Training Type:
Swim ◯ Dryland ◯ Other ◯

Weather:

TRAINING SESSION
Nº of laps: .... Distance Swum: ....

WARM-UP   MAIN SET   COOL-DOWN
INTERVALS   SPRINTS   DIVES   STARTS   TURNS
DRILLS   PULL BUOY   FINS   OTHER

Mood Tracker
Pre-workout:
Post-workout:

Thoughts & Reflections

Did I get enough...
water   sleep
Y N   Y N

Meals	Today I ate:
• BREAKFAST	
• LUNCH	
• DINNER	
• SNACKS	

Total Time Spent In The Water: ....
Rate today's workout: /10

TRAINING ENERGY LEVELS
Before   After

Best part about today was ...

Feedback...

Today's Goal:

Powered by
Chlorine
SWIM LOGBOOK

Coach:

Location:

Pool: 25 ◯ 50 ◯ Other ◯

Training Type:
Swim ◯ Dryland ◯ Other ◯

Time:

Date: / /20

S M T W T F S

Weather: ☀ ⛅ 🌧 🌦 ❄

TRAINING SESSION
Nº of laps: .... Distance Swum: ....

WARM-UP   MAIN SET   COOL-DOWN
INTERVALS   SPRINTS   DIVES   STARTS   TURNS
DRILLS   PULL BUOY   FINS   OTHER

Total Time Spent In The Water: ....
Rate today's workout: /10

Mood Tracker
Pre-workout: 😊 😳 😐 🤪 😣 😠 😎
Post-workout: 😊 😳 😐 🤪 😣 😠 😎

Thoughts & Reflections

Did I get enough...
water Y N   sleep Y N

Meals	Today I ate:
• BREAKFAST	
• LUNCH	
• DINNER	
• SNACKS	

TRAINING ENERGY LEVELS
Before   After

Best part about today was ...

Feedback...

Today's Goal:

Powered by
Chlorine
SWIM LOGBOOK

Coach:

Location:

Pool:
25 ◯   50 ◯   Other ◯

Time:

Date: /   /20

S M T W T F S

Weather: ☀ ⛅ 🌦 ☁ ❄

Training Type:
Swim ◯   Dryland ◯   Other ◯

TRAINING SESSION
Nº of laps: ....   Distance Swum: ....

WARM-UP   MAIN SET   COOL-DOWN
INTERVALS   SPRINTS   DIVES   STARTS   TURNS
DRILLS   PULL BUOY   FINS   OTHER

Mood Tracker
Pre-workout: 😊 😅 😐 😖 😠 😎
Post-workout: 😊 😅 😐 😖 😠 😎

Thoughts & Reflections

Did I get enough...
water   sleep
Y N   Y N

Meals	Today I ate:
• BREAKFAST	
• LUNCH	
• DINNER	
• SNACKS	

Total Time Spent In The Water: ....
Rate today's workout: /10

TRAINING ENERGY LEVELS
Before   After

Best part about today was ...

Feedback...

Today's Goal:

Powered by
Chlorine
SWIM LOGBOOK

Coach:

Location:

Pool:
25 ◯ 50 ◯ Other ◯

Training Type:
Swim ◯ Dryland ◯ Other ◯

Time:

Date: / /20

S M T W T F S

Weather:
☀ ⛅ 🌧 🌩 ❄

TRAINING SESSION
Nº of laps: .... Distance Swum: ....

WARM-UP   MAIN SET   COOL-DOWN
INTERVALS   SPRINTS   DIVES   STARTS   TURNS
DRILLS   PULL BUOY   FINS   OTHER

Total Time Spent In The Water: ....
Rate today's workout: /10

Mood Tracker
Pre-workout: 😊 😴 😐 😜 😣 😎
Post-workout: 😊 😴 😐 😜 😣 😎

Thoughts & Reflections
....
....
....
....
....
....
....

Did I get enough...
water   sleep
Y N   Y N

Meals	Today I ate:
• BREAKFAST	
• LUNCH	
• DINNER	
• SNACKS	

TRAINING ENERGY LEVELS
Before   After

Best part about today was ...

Feedback...

Today's Goal:

Powered by
Chlorine
SWIM LOGBOOK

Coach:

Location:

Time:

Date: / /20

S M T W T F S

Pool:
25 ◯ 50 ◯ Other ◯

Training Type:
Swim ◯ Dryland ◯ Other ◯

Weather: ☀ ⛅ 🌥 🌧 ❄

TRAINING SESSION
Nº of laps: .... Distance Swum: ....

WARM-UP   MAIN SET   COOL-DOWN
INTERVALS   SPRINTS   DIVES   STARTS   TURNS
DRILLS   PULL BUOY   FINS   OTHER

Total Time Spent In The Water: ....
Rate today's workout: /10

Mood Tracker
Pre-workout: 😊 😐 😕 🤔 😣 😎
Post-workout: 😊 😐 😕 🤔 😣 😎

Thoughts & Reflections
....
....
....
....
....
....
....

Did I get enough...
water   sleep
Y N   Y N

Meals	Today I ate:
• BREAKFAST	
• LUNCH	
• DINNER	
• SNACKS	

TRAINING ENERGY LEVELS
Before   After

Best part about today was ...

Feedback...

Today's Goal:

Powered by
Chlorine
SWIM LOGBOOK

Coach:

Location:

Pool: 25 ◯ 50 ◯ Other ◯

Time:

Date: / /20

S M T W T F S

Weather: ☀ ⛅ 🌥 🌧 ❄

Training Type:
Swim ◯ Dryland ◯ Other ◯

TRAINING SESSION
Nº of laps: .... Distance Swum: ....

WARM-UP MAIN SET COOL-DOWN
INTERVALS SPRINTS DIVES STARTS TURNS
DRILLS PULL BUOY FINS OTHER

Mood Tracker
Pre-workout: 😊 😳 😐 😤 😠 😢 😎
Post-workout: 😊 😳 😐 😤 😠 😢 😎

Thoughts & Reflections
_____
_____
_____
_____
_____

Did I get enough...
water Y N   sleep Y N

Meals	Today I ate:
• BREAKFAST	
• LUNCH	
• DINNER	
• SNACKS	

Total Time Spent In The Water: ....
Rate today's workout: /10

TRAINING ENERGY LEVELS
Before   After

Best part about today was ...

Feedback...

Today's Goal:

Powered by
Chlorine
SWIM LOGBOOK

Coach:

Location:

Pool:
25 ◯ 50 ◯ Other ◯

Time:

Date: ___ / ___ /20___

S M T W T F S

Training Type:
Swim ◯ Dryland ◯ Other ◯

Weather:

TRAINING SESSION
Nº of laps: .... Distance Swum: ....
WARM-UP   MAIN SET   COOL-DOWN
INTERVALS SPRINTS DIVES STARTS TURNS
DRILLS PULL BUOY FINS OTHER

Mood Tracker
Pre-workout:
Post-workout:

Thoughts & Reflections
....
....
....
....
....

Did I get enough...
water   sleep
Y N   Y N

Meals	Today I ate:
• BREAKFAST	
• LUNCH	
• DINNER	
• SNACKS	

Total Time Spent In The Water: ....
Rate today's workout: _____ /10

TRAINING ENERGY LEVELS
Before | After

Best part about today was ...

Feedback...

Today's Goal:

Powered by
CHLORINE
SWIM LOGBOOK

Coach:

Location:

Pool: 25 ◯ 50 ◯ Other ◯

Training Type:
Swim ◯ Dryland ◯ Other ◯

Time:

Date: / /20

S M T W T F S

Weather: ☀ ⛅ 🌧 ☁ ❄

TRAINING SESSION
Nº of laps: .... Distance Swum: ....

WARM-UP MAIN SET COOL-DOWN
INTERVALS SPRINTS DIVES STARTS TURNS
DRILLS PULL BUOY FINS OTHER

Total Time Spent In The Water: ....
Rate today's workout: /10

Mood Tracker
Pre-workout: 🙂 😳 😐 🥴 😠 😣 😎
Post-workout: 🙂 😳 😐 🥴 😠 😣 😎

Thoughts & Reflections
....
....
....
....
....
....
....

Did I get enough...
water Y N   sleep Y N

Meals	Today I ate:
• BREAKFAST	
• LUNCH	
• DINNER	
• SNACKS	

TRAINING ENERGY LEVELS
Before After

Best part about today was ...

Feedback...

Today's Goal:

Powered by
Chlorine
SWIM LOGBOOK

Coach:

Location:

Pool: 25 ◯ 50 ◯ Other ◯

Time:

Date: /   /20

S M T W T F S

Weather: ☀ ⛅ 🌦 ☁ ❄

Training Type:
Swim ◯ Dryland ◯ Other ◯

TRAINING SESSION
Nº of laps: .... Distance Swum: ....
WARM-UP   MAIN SET   COOL-DOWN
INTERVALS   SPRINTS   DIVES   STARTS   TURNS
DRILLS   PULL BUOY   FINS   OTHER

Total Time Spent In The Water: ....
Rate today's workout: /10

Mood Tracker
Pre-workout: 😊 😳 😂 😠 😡 😎
Post-workout: 😊 😳 😐 😂 😠 😡 😎

Thoughts & Reflections
_____
_____
_____
_____
_____
_____
_____

Did I get enough...
water   sleep
Y N   Y N

Meals	Today I ate:
• BREAKFAST	
• LUNCH	
• DINNER	
• SNACKS	

TRAINING ENERGY LEVELS
Before   After

Best part about today was ...

Feedback...

Today's Goal:

Powered by
Chlorine
SWIM LOGBOOK

Coach:

Time:

Location:

Date: / /20

S M T W T F S

Pool:
25 ○ 50 ○ Other ○

Weather:

Training Type:
Swim ○ Dryland ○ Other ○

TRAINING SESSION
Nº of laps: .... Distance Swum: ....

WARM-UP MAIN SET COOL-DOWN
INTERVALS SPRINTS DIVES STARTS TURNS
DRILLS PULL BUOY FINS OTHER

Mood Tracker
Pre-workout: 😊 😵 😌 🤪 😣 😎
Post-workout: 😊 😵 😌 🤪 😣 😎

Thoughts & Reflections

Did I get enough...
water sleep
Y N   Y N

Meals	Today I ate:
• BREAKFAST	
• LUNCH	
• DINNER	
• SNACKS	

Total Time Spent In The Water: ....
Rate today's workout: /10

TRAINING ENERGY LEVELS
Before   After

Best part about today was ...

Feedback...

Today's Goal:

Powered by
Chlorine
SWIM LOGBOOK

Coach:

Location:

Time:

Date: /   /20

S M T W T F S

Pool:
25 ◯ 50 ◯ Other ◯

Training Type:
Swim ◯ Dryland ◯ Other ◯

Weather:

TRAINING SESSION
Nº of laps: .... Distance Swum: ....

WARM-UP   MAIN SET   COOL-DOWN
INTERVALS   SPRINTS   DIVES   STARTS   TURNS
DRILLS   PULL BUOY   FINS   OTHER

Mood Tracker
Pre-workout: 😊 😳 😐 😉 😖 😎
Post-workout: 😊 😟 😐 😉 😣 😎

Thoughts & Reflections

Did I get enough...
water   sleep
Y N   Y N

Meals	Today I ate:
• BREAKFAST	
• LUNCH	
• DINNER	
• SNACKS	

Total Time Spent In The Water: ....
Rate today's workout: /10

TRAINING ENERGY LEVELS
Before   After

Best part about today was ...

Feedback...

Today's Goal:

Powered by
Chlorine
SWIM LOGBOOK

Coach:

Location:

Pool:
25 ◯ 50 ◯ Other ◯

Training Type:
Swim ◯ Dryland ◯ Other ◯

Time:

Date: / /20

S M T W T F S

Weather:

TRAINING SESSION
Nº of laps: .... Distance Swum: ....

WARM-UP   MAIN SET   COOL-DOWN
INTERVALS   SPRINTS   DIVES   STARTS   TURNS
DRILLS   PULL BUOY   FINS   OTHER

Total Time Spent In The Water: ....
Rate today's workout: /10

Mood Tracker
Pre-workout:
Post-workout:

Thoughts & Reflections

Did I get enough...
water   sleep
Y N   Y N

Meals	Today I ate:
• BREAKFAST	
• LUNCH	
• DINNER	
• SNACKS	

TRAINING ENERGY LEVELS
Before   After

Best part about today was ...

Feedback...

Today's Goal:

Powered by
Chlorine
SWIM LOGBOOK

Coach:

Location:

Pool:
25 ○ 50 ○ Other ○

Time:

Date: / /20

S M T W T F S

Weather:

Training Type:
Swim ○ Dryland ○ Other ○

TRAINING SESSION
Nº of laps: .... Distance Swum: ....
WARM-UP   MAIN SET   COOL-DOWN
INTERVALS   SPRINTS   DIVES   STARTS   TURNS
DRILLS   PULL BUOY   FINS   OTHER

Mood Tracker
Pre-workout:
Post-workout:

Thoughts & Reflections

Did I get enough...
water   sleep
Y N   Y N

Meals	Today I ate:
• BREAKFAST	
• LUNCH	
• DINNER	
• SNACKS	

Total Time Spent In The Water: ....
Rate today's workout: /10

TRAINING ENERGY LEVELS
Before   After

Best part about today was ...

Feedback...

Today's Goal:

Powered by
ChloRiNe
SWIM LOGBOOK

Coach:

Location:

Pool:
25 ◯ 50 ◯ Other ◯

Time:

Date: / /20

S M T W T F S

Weather:

Training Type:
Swim ◯ Dryland ◯ Other ◯

TRAINING SESSION
Nº of laps: .... Distance Swum: ....

WARM-UP MAIN SET COOL-DOWN
INTERVALS SPRINTS DIVES STARTS TURNS
DRILLS PULL BUOY FINS OTHER

Mood Tracker
Pre-workout: 😊 😳 😐 🤪 ☹️ 😎
Post-workout: 😊 😳 😐 🤪 ☹️ 😎

Thoughts & Reflections

Did I get enough...
water   sleep
Y N   Y N

Meals	Today I ate:
• BREAKFAST	
• LUNCH	
• DINNER	
• SNACKS	

Total Time Spent In The Water: ....
Rate today's workout: /10

TRAINING ENERGY LEVELS
Before   After

Best part about today was ...

Feedback...

Today's Goal:

Powered by
Chlorine
SWIM LOGBOOK

Coach:

Location:

Pool: 25 ◯ 50 ◯ Other ◯

Time:

Date: / /20

S M T W T F S

Weather: ☀ ☁ 🌦 🌧 ❄

Training Type:
Swim ◯ Dryland ◯ Other ◯

TRAINING SESSION
Nº of laps: .... Distance Swum: ....

WARM-UP   MAIN SET   COOL-DOWN
INTERVALS   SPRINTS   DIVES   STARTS   TURNS
DRILLS   PULL BUOY   FINS   OTHER

Total Time Spent In The Water: ....
Rate today's workout: /10

Mood Tracker
Pre-workout: 😊 😅 😐 🤪 😣 😎
Post-workout: 😊 😅 😐 🤪 😣 😎

Thoughts & Reflections

Did I get enough...
water   Y N
sleep   Y N

Meals	Today I ate:
• BREAKFAST	
• LUNCH	
• DINNER	
• SNACKS	

TRAINING ENERGY LEVELS
Before   After

Best part about today was ...

Feedback...

Today's Goal:

Powered by
Chlorine
SWIM LOGBOOK

Coach:

Location:

Pool: 25 ○ 50 ○ Other ○

Time:

Date: / /20

S M T W T F S

Weather: ☀️ ☁️ 🌦️ 🌧️ ❄️

Training Type:
Swim ○ Dryland ○ Other ○

TRAINING SESSION
Nº of laps: .... Distance Swum: ....

WARM-UP MAIN SET COOL-DOWN
INTERVALS SPRINTS DIVES STARTS TURNS
DRILLS PULL BUOY FINS OTHER

Total Time Spent In The Water: ....
Rate today's workout: /10

Mood Tracker
Pre-workout: 😊 😴 😐 🤪 😣 ☹️ 😎
Post-workout: 😊 😴 😐 🤪 😣 ☹️ 😎

Thoughts & Reflections
_____
_____
_____
_____
_____
_____

Did I get enough...
water Y N   sleep Y N

Meals	Today I ate:
• BREAKFAST	
• LUNCH	
• DINNER	
• SNACKS	

TRAINING ENERGY LEVELS
Before   After

Best part about today was ...

Feedback...

Today's Goal:

Powered by
Chlorine
SWIM LOGBOOK

Coach:

Time:

Location:

Date: / /20

S M T W T F S

Pool:
25 ◯ 50 ◯ Other ◯

Training Type:
Swim ◯ Dryland ◯ Other ◯

Weather: ☀ ⛅ 🌦 🌧 ❄

TRAINING SESSION
Nº of laps: .... Distance Swum: ....

WARM-UP   MAIN SET   COOL-DOWN
INTERVALS   SPRINTS   DIVES   STARTS   TURNS
DRILLS   PULL BUOY   FINS   OTHER

Mood Tracker
Pre-workout: 🙂 😬 😐 🤔 😣 😎
Post-workout: 🙂 😬 😐 🤔 😣 😎

Thoughts & Reflections
....
....
....
....
....
....

Did I get enough...
water   sleep
Y N   Y N

Meals	Today I ate:
• BREAKFAST	
• LUNCH	
• DINNER	
• SNACKS	

Total Time Spent In The Water: ....
Rate today's workout: /10

TRAINING ENERGY LEVELS
Before   After

Best part about today was ...

Feedback...

Today's Goal:

Powered by
Chlorine
SWIM LOGBOOK

Coach:

Location:

Pool:
25 ○ 50 ○ Other ○

Training Type:
Swim ○ Dryland ○ Other ○

Time:

Date: / /20

S M T W T F S

Weather:

TRAINING SESSION
Nº of laps: .... Distance Swum: ....

WARM-UP MAIN SET COOL-DOWN
INTERVALS SPRINTS DIVES STARTS TURNS
DRILLS PULL BUOY FINS OTHER

Total Time Spent In The Water: ....
Rate today's workout: /10

Mood Tracker
Pre-workout:
Post-workout:

Thoughts & Reflections

Did I get enough...
water   sleep
Y N   Y N

Meals	Today I ate:
• BREAKFAST	
• LUNCH	
• DINNER	
• SNACKS	

TRAINING ENERGY LEVELS
Before   After

Best part about today was ...

Feedback...

Today's Goal:

Powered by
Chlorine
SWIM LOGBOOK

Coach:

Time:

Location:

Date: / /20

S M T W T F S

Pool:
25 ◯ 50 ◯ Other ◯

Training Type:
Swim ◯ Dryland ◯ Other ◯

Weather:

TRAINING SESSION
Nº of laps: .... Distance Swum: ....

WARM-UP MAIN SET COOL-DOWN
INTERVALS SPRINTS DIVES STARTS TURNS
DRILLS PULL BUOY FINS OTHER

Total Time Spent In The Water: ....
Rate today's workout: /10

Mood Tracker
Pre-workout:
Post-workout:

Thoughts & Reflections

Did I get enough...
water Y N
sleep Y N

Meals	Today I ate:
• BREAKFAST	
• LUNCH	
• DINNER	
• SNACKS	

TRAINING ENERGY LEVELS
Before After

Best part about today was ...

Feedback...

Today's Goal:

Powered by
Chlorine
SWIM LOGBOOK

Coach:

Location:

Pool: 25 ◯ 50 ◯ Other ◯

Training Type:
Swim ◯ Dryland ◯ Other ◯

Time:

Date: / /20

S M T W T F S

Weather: ☀ ⛅ 🌧 ❄

TRAINING SESSION
Nº of laps: .... Distance Swum: ....

WARM-UP MAIN SET COOL-DOWN
INTERVALS SPRINTS DIVES STARTS TURNS
DRILLS PULL BUOY FINS OTHER

Total Time Spent In The Water: ....
Rate today's workout: /10

Mood Tracker
Pre-workout: 😊 😐 🙂 😤 😠 😎
Post-workout: 😊 😐 🙂 😤 😠 😎

Thoughts & Reflections
_____
_____
_____
_____
_____
_____

Did I get enough...
water Y N   sleep Y N

Meals	Today I ate:
• BREAKFAST	
• LUNCH	
• DINNER	
• SNACKS	

TRAINING ENERGY LEVELS
Before   After

Best part about today was ...

Feedback...

Today's Goal:

Powered by
Chlorine
SWIM LOGBOOK

Coach:

Time:

Location:

Date: ___ / ___ /20___

S M T W T F S

Pool:
25 ◯   50 ◯   Other ◯

Weather: ☀️ ⛅ 🌦️ 🌧️ ❄️

Training Type:
Swim ◯   Dryland ◯   Other ◯

TRAINING SESSION
Nº of laps: ....   Distance Swum: ....

WARM-UP   MAIN SET   COOL-DOWN
INTERVALS   SPRINTS   DIVES   STARTS   TURNS
DRILLS   PULL BUOY   FINS   OTHER

Mood Tracker
Pre-workout: 🙂 😀 😐 😣 😠 😎
Post-workout: 🙂 😀 😐 😣 😠 😎

Thoughts & Reflections

Did I get enough...
water   sleep
Y N   Y N

Meals	Today I ate:
• BREAKFAST	
• LUNCH	
• DINNER	
• SNACKS	

Total Time Spent In The Water: ....
Rate today's workout: /10

TRAINING ENERGY LEVELS
Before   After

Best part about today was ...

Feedback...

Today's Goal:

Powered by Chlorine
SWIM LOGBOOK

Coach:

Location:

Pool:
25 ○ 50 ○ Other ○

Time:

Date: /   /20

S M T W T F S

Weather:

Training Type:
Swim ○ Dryland ○ Other ○

TRAINING SESSION
Nº of laps: .... Distance Swum: ....

WARM-UP MAIN SET COOL-DOWN
INTERVALS SPRINTS DIVES STARTS TURNS
DRILLS PULL BUOY FINS OTHER

Mood Tracker
Pre-workout: 😊 😳 😐 😜 😣 😎
Post-workout: 😊 😳 😐 😜 😣 😎

Thoughts & Reflections

Did I get enough...
water   sleep
Y N   Y N

Meals	Today I ate:
• BREAKFAST	
• LUNCH	
• DINNER	
• SNACKS	

Total Time Spent In The Water: ....
Rate today's workout: /10

TRAINING ENERGY LEVELS
Before   After

Best part about today was ...

Feedback...

Today's Goal:

Powered by
Chlorine
SWIM LOGBOOK

Coach:

Location:

Pool: 25 ◯ 50 ◯ Other ◯

Time:

Date: /   /20

S M T W T F S

Weather: ☀ ⛅ 🌦 ☁ ❄

Training Type:
Swim ◯ Dryland ◯ Other ◯

TRAINING SESSION
Nº of laps: .... Distance Swum: ....

WARM-UP   MAIN SET   COOL-DOWN
INTERVALS   SPRINTS   DIVES   STARTS   TURNS
DRILLS   PULL BUOY   FINS   OTHER

Mood Tracker
Pre-workout: 😊 😀 😐 🤪 😣 😎
Post-workout: 😊 😀 😐 🤪 😣 😎

Thoughts & Reflections

Did I get enough...
water   Y N   sleep   Y N

Meals	Today I ate:
• BREAKFAST	
• LUNCH	
• DINNER	
• SNACKS	

Total Time Spent In The Water: ....
Rate today's workout: /10

TRAINING ENERGY LEVELS
Before   After

Best part about today was ...

Feedback...

Today's Goal:

Powered by
CHLORINE
SWIM LOGBOOK

Coach:

Location:

Time:

Date: __ / __ /20__

S M T W T F S

Pool:
25 ◯ 50 ◯ Other ◯

Training Type:
Swim ◯ Dryland ◯ Other ◯

Weather:

TRAINING SESSION
Nº of laps: .... Distance Swum: ....

WARM-UP   MAIN SET   COOL-DOWN
INTERVALS   SPRINTS   DIVES   STARTS   TURNS
DRILLS   PULL BUOY   FINS   OTHER

Mood Tracker
Pre-workout:
Post-workout:

Thoughts & Reflections

Did I get enough...
water   Y N
sleep   Y N

Meals	Today I ate:
• BREAKFAST	
• LUNCH	
• DINNER	
• SNACKS	

Total Time Spent In The Water: ....
Rate today's workout: /10

TRAINING ENERGY LEVELS
Before   After

Best part about today was ...

Feedback...

Today's Goal:

Powered by Chlorine
SWIM LOGBOOK

Coach:

Time:

Location:

Date: / /20

S M T W T F S

Training Type:
Swim ○ Dryland ○ Other ○

Pool:
25 ○ 50 ○ Other ○

Weather: ☀ ⛅ 🌦 ☁ ❄

TRAINING SESSION
Nº of laps: .... Distance Swum: ....

WARM-UP   MAIN SET   COOL-DOWN
INTERVALS SPRINTS DIVES STARTS TURNS
DRILLS PULL BUOY FINS OTHER

Mood Tracker
Pre-workout: 😀 😐 🤣 😣 😠 😎
Post-workout: 😀 😕 😂 😖 😫 😎

Thoughts & Reflections

Did I get enough...
water Y N   💤 sleep Y N

Meals	Today I ate:
• BREAKFAST	
• LUNCH	
• DINNER	
• SNACKS	

Total Time Spent In The Water: ....
Rate today's workout: /10

TRAINING ENERGY LEVELS
Before   After

Best part about today was ...

Feedback...

Today's Goal:

Powered by
Chlorine
SWIM LOGBOOK

Coach:

Location:

Pool: 25 ◯ 50 ◯ Other ◯

Training Type:
Swim ◯ Dryland ◯ Other ◯

Time:

Date: ___ / ___ /20___

S M T W T F S

Weather:

TRAINING SESSION
N° of laps: .... Distance Swum: ....

WARM-UP MAIN SET COOL-DOWN
INTERVALS SPRINTS DIVES STARTS TURNS
DRILLS PULL BUOY FINS OTHER

Total Time Spent In The Water: ....
Rate today's workout: ___ /10

Mood Tracker
Pre-workout:
Post-workout:

Thoughts & Reflections

Did I get enough...
water Y N
sleep Y N

Meals	Today I ate:
• BREAKFAST	
• LUNCH	
• DINNER	
• SNACKS	

TRAINING ENERGY LEVELS
Before   After

Best part about today was ...

Feedback...

Today's Goal:

Powered by
Chlorine
SWIM LOGBOOK

Coach:

Time:

Location:

Date: /   /20

S M T W T F S

Pool:
25 ◯   50 ◯   Other ◯

Weather: ☀ ⛅ 🌦 🌧 ❄

Training Type:
Swim ◯   Dryland ◯   Other ◯

TRAINING SESSION
Nº of laps: ....   Distance Swum: ....

WARM-UP   MAIN SET   COOL-DOWN
INTERVALS   SPRINTS   DIVES   STARTS   TURNS
DRILLS   PULL BUOY   FINS   OTHER

Mood Tracker
Pre-workout: 😊 😓 😐 😫 😠 😎
Post-workout: 😊 😓 😐 😫 😠 😎

Thoughts & Reflections

Did I get enough...
water   sleep
Y N   Y N

Meals	Today I ate:
• BREAKFAST	
• LUNCH	
• DINNER	
• SNACKS	

Total Time Spent In The Water: ....
Rate today's workout: /10

TRAINING ENERGY LEVELS
Before   After

Best part about today was ...

Feedback...

Today's Goal:

Powered by
Chlorine
SWIM LOGBOOK

Coach:

Location:

Pool:
25 ◯ 50 ◯ Other ◯

Training Type:
Swim ◯ Dryland ◯ Other ◯

Time:

Date: / /20
S M T W T F S

Weather:
☀ ☁ 🌧 🌧 ❄

TRAINING SESSION
Nº of laps: .... Distance Swum: ....

WARM-UP MAIN SET COOL-DOWN
INTERVALS SPRINTS DIVES STARTS TURNS
DRILLS PULL BUOY FINS OTHER

Total Time Spent In The Water: ....
Rate today's workout: /10

Mood Tracker
Pre-workout: 😊 🤢 😐 🤪 😣 😠 😎
Post-workout: 😊 🤢 😐 🤪 😣 😠 😎

Thoughts & Reflections

Did I get enough...
water   sleep
Y N   Y N

Meals	Today I ate:
• BREAKFAST	
• LUNCH	
• DINNER	
• SNACKS	

TRAINING ENERGY LEVELS
Before   After

Best part about today was ...

Feedback...

Today's Goal:

Powered by
Chlorine
SWIM LOGBOOK

Coach:

Location:

Pool: 25 ◯ 50 ◯ Other ◯

Time:

Date: / /20

S M T W T F S

Weather: ☀ ⛅ 🌥 🌧 ❄

Training Type:
Swim ◯ Dryland ◯ Other ◯

TRAINING SESSION
Nº of laps: .... Distance Swum: ....

WARM-UP   MAIN SET   COOL-DOWN
INTERVALS   SPRINTS   DIVES   STARTS   TURNS
DRILLS   PULL BUOY   FINS   OTHER

Total Time Spent In The Water: ....
Rate today's workout: /10

Mood Tracker
Pre-workout: 😊 😦 😐 🤔 😣 😎
Post-workout: 😊 😦 😐 🤔 😣 😎

Thoughts & Reflections

Did I get enough...
water   Y N   sleep   Y N

Meals	Today I ate:
• BREAKFAST	
• LUNCH	
• DINNER	
• SNACKS	

TRAINING ENERGY LEVELS
Before   After

Best part about today was ...

Feedback...

Today's Goal:

Powered by
Chlorine
SWIM LOGBOOK

Coach:

Location:

Pool: 25 ◯ 50 ◯ Other ◯

Time:

Date: ___ / ___ /20

S M T W T F S

Weather: ☀ ⛅ 🌧 ☁ ❄

Training Type:
Swim ◯ Dryland ◯ Other ◯

TRAINING SESSION
Nº of laps: .... Distance Swum: ....

WARM-UP MAIN SET COOL-DOWN
INTERVALS SPRINTS DIVES STARTS TURNS
DRILLS PULL BUOY FINS OTHER

Total Time Spent In The Water: ....
Rate today's workout: ___/10

Mood Tracker
Pre-workout: 😊 😳 😐 🤪 😠 😎
Post-workout: 😊 😳 😐 🤪 😠 😎

Thoughts & Reflections

Did I get enough...
water Y N   sleep Y N

Meals	Today I ate:
• BREAKFAST	
• LUNCH	
• DINNER	
• SNACKS	

TRAINING ENERGY LEVELS
Before After

Best part about today was ...

Feedback...

Today's Goal:

Powered by
Chlorine
SWIM LOGBOOK

Coach:

Location:

Pool:
25 ◯   50 ◯   Other ◯

Time:

Date: /   /20

S M T W T F S

Weather:
☀ ⛅ 🌦 ☁ ❄

Training Type:
Swim ◯ Dryland ◯ Other ◯

TRAINING SESSION
Nº of laps: ....   Distance Swum: ....

WARM-UP   MAIN SET   COOL-DOWN
INTERVALS   SPRINTS   DIVES   STARTS   TURNS
DRILLS   PULL BUOY   FINS   OTHER

Total Time Spent In The Water: ....
Rate today's workout: /10

Mood Tracker
Pre-workout: 😊 😄 😐 😣 😠 😎
Post-workout: 😊 😄 😐 😣 😠 😎

Thoughts & Reflections
_____
_____
_____
_____
_____

Did I get enough...
water   sleep
Y N   Y N

Meals	Today I ate:
• BREAKFAST	
• LUNCH	
• DINNER	
• SNACKS	

TRAINING ENERGY LEVELS
Before   After

Best part about today was ...

Feedback...

Today's Goal:

Powered by
Chlorine
SWIM LOGBOOK

Coach:

Time:

Location:

Date: ___ / ___ /20___

S M T W T F S

Pool:
25 ◯ 50 ◯ Other ◯

Weather: ☀ ☁ 🌦 🌧 ❄

Training Type:
Swim ◯ Dryland ◯ Other ◯

TRAINING SESSION
Nº of laps: .... Distance Swum: ....

WARM-UP MAIN SET COOL-DOWN
INTERVALS SPRINTS DIVES STARTS TURNS
DRILLS PULL BUOY FINS OTHER

Mood Tracker
Pre-workout: 😊 😨 😐 🤢 😠 😎
Post-workout: 😊 😨 😐 🤢 😠 😎

Thoughts & Reflections
....
....
....
....
....
....

Did I get enough...
water   sleep
Y N   Y N

Meals	Today I ate:
• BREAKFAST	
• LUNCH	
• DINNER	
• SNACKS	

Total Time Spent In The Water: ....
Rate today's workout: /10

TRAINING ENERGY LEVELS
Before   After

Best part about today was ...

Feedback...

Today's Goal:

Powered by
Chlorine
SWIM LOGBOOK

Coach:

Time:

Location:

Date: / /20

S M T W T F S

Pool:
25 ◯ 50 ◯ Other ◯

Training Type:
Swim ◯ Dryland ◯ Other ◯

Weather: ☀️ ⛅ 🌥️ 🌧️ ❄️

TRAINING SESSION
Nº of laps: .... Distance Swum: ....

WARM-UP   MAIN SET   COOL-DOWN
INTERVALS   SPRINTS   DIVES   STARTS   TURNS
DRILLS   PULL BUOY   FINS   OTHER

Mood Tracker
Pre-workout: 🙂 😀 🤣 😠 😡 😎
Post-workout: 🙂 😀 🤣 😠 😡 😎

Thoughts & Reflections

Did I get enough...
water   sleep
Y N   Y N

Meals	Today I ate:
• BREAKFAST	
• LUNCH	
• DINNER	
• SNACKS	

Total Time Spent In The Water: ....
Rate today's workout: /10

TRAINING ENERGY LEVELS
Before   After

Best part about today was ...

Feedback...

Today's Goal:

Powered by
Chlorine
SWIM LOGBOOK

Coach:

Location:

Time:

Date: / /20

S M T W T F S

Pool:
25 ◯ 50 ◯ Other ◯

Training Type:
Swim ◯ Dryland ◯ Other ◯

Weather:

TRAINING SESSION
Nº of laps: .... Distance Swum: ....

WARM-UP MAIN SET COOL-DOWN
INTERVALS SPRINTS DIVES STARTS TURNS
DRILLS PULL BUOY FINS OTHER

Mood Tracker
Pre-workout:
Post-workout:

Thoughts & Reflections

Did I get enough...
water sleep
Y N Y N

Meals	Today I ate:
• BREAKFAST	
• LUNCH	
• DINNER	
• SNACKS	

Total Time Spent In The Water: ....
Rate today's workout: /10

TRAINING ENERGY LEVELS
Before After

Best part about today was ...

Feedback...

Today's Goal:

Powered by
Chlorine
SWIM **LOGBOOK**

Coach:

Location:

Pool:
25 ◯ 50 ◯ Other ◯

Time:

Date: / /20

S M T W T F S

Weather: ☀ ⛅ 🌤 ☁ 🌧 ❄

Training Type:
Swim ◯ Dryland ◯ Other ◯

TRAINING SESSION
Nº of laps: .... Distance Swum: ....

WARM-UP   MAIN SET   COOL-DOWN
INTERVALS   SPRINTS   DIVES   STARTS   TURNS
DRILLS   PULL BUOY   FINS   OTHER

Mood Tracker
Pre-workout: 😊 😖 😐 😉 😣 😎
Post-workout: 😊 😖 😐 😉 😣 😎

Thoughts & Reflections

Did I get enough...
water   sleep
Y N   Y N

Meals	Today I ate:
• BREAKFAST	
• LUNCH	
• DINNER	
• SNACKS	

Total Time Spent In The Water: ....
Rate today's workout: /10

TRAINING ENERGY LEVELS
Before   After

Best part about today was ...

Feedback...

Today's Goal:

Powered by Chlorine
SWIM LOGBOOK

Coach:

Location:

Pool: 25 ◯ 50 ◯ Other ◯

Time:

Date: ___ / ___ /20___

S M T W T F S

Weather: ☀ ⛅ 🌧 🌦 ❄

Training Type:
Swim ◯ Dryland ◯ Other ◯

TRAINING SESSION
Nº of laps: .... Distance Swum: ....

WARM-UP   MAIN SET   COOL-DOWN
INTERVALS   SPRINTS   DIVES   STARTS   TURNS
DRILLS   PULL BUOY   FINS   OTHER

Mood Tracker
Pre-workout: 😊 😨 😐 😡 😠 😎
Post-workout: 😊 😨 😐 😡 😠 😎

Thoughts & Reflections
_____
_____
_____
_____
_____
_____

Did I get enough...
water   Y N   sleep   Y N

Meals	Today I ate:
• BREAKFAST	
• LUNCH	
• DINNER	
• SNACKS	

Total Time Spent In The Water: ....
Rate today's workout: /10

TRAINING ENERGY LEVELS
Before   After

Best part about today was ...

Feedback...

Today's Goal:

Powered by
Chlorine
SWIM LOGBOOK

Coach:

Location:

Pool:
25 ○ 50 ○ Other ○

Time:

Date: / /20

S M T W T F S

Weather: ☀️ ⛅ 🌧️ ☁️ ❄️

Training Type:
Swim ○ Dryland ○ Other ○

TRAINING SESSION
Nº of laps: .... Distance Swum: ....

WARM-UP MAIN SET COOL-DOWN
INTERVALS SPRINTS DIVES STARTS TURNS
DRILLS PULL BUOY FINS OTHER

Mood Tracker
Pre-workout: 😴 😀 🤪 😐 😠 😎
Post-workout: 😴 😀 🤪 😐 😠 😎

Thoughts & Reflections

Did I get enough...
water sleep
Y N   Y N

Meals	Today I ate:
• BREAKFAST	
• LUNCH	
• DINNER	
• SNACKS	

Total Time Spent In The Water: ....
Rate today's workout: /10

TRAINING ENERGY LEVELS
Before After

Best part about today was ...

Feedback...

Today's Goal:

Powered by
Chlorine
SWIM LOGBOOK

Coach:

Location:

Pool:
25 ◯ 50 ◯ Other ◯

Training Type:
Swim ◯ Dryland ◯ Other ◯

Time:

Date: /   /20

S M T W T F S

Weather: ☀ ⛅ 🌦 🌧 ❄

TRAINING SESSION
Nº of laps: .... Distance Swum: ....

WARM-UP MAIN SET COOL-DOWN
INTERVALS SPRINTS DIVES STARTS TURNS
DRILLS PULL BUOY FINS OTHER

Total Time Spent In The Water: ....
Rate today's workout: /10

Mood Tracker
Pre-workout: 😊 😨 😐 🥴 😠 🙁 😎
Post-workout: 😊 😨 😐 🥴 😠 🙁 😎

Thoughts & Reflections
....
....
....
....
....
....
....

Did I get enough...
water   sleep
Y N   zZz   Y N

Meals	Today I ate:
• BREAKFAST	
• LUNCH	
• DINNER	
• SNACKS	

TRAINING ENERGY LEVELS
Before   After

Best part about today was ...

Feedback...

Today's Goal:

Powered by Chlorine
SWIM LOGBOOK

Coach:

Location:

Pool: 25 ○ 50 ○ Other ○

Training Type:
Swim ○ Dryland ○ Other ○

Time:

Date: ___ / ___ /20___

S M T W T F S

Weather: ☀️ ⛅ 🌧️ ☁️ ❄️

TRAINING SESSION
Nº of laps: .... Distance Swum: ....

WARM-UP   MAIN SET   COOL-DOWN
INTERVALS   SPRINTS   DIVES   STARTS   TURNS
DRILLS   PULL BUOY   FINS   OTHER

Total Time Spent In The Water: ....
Rate today's workout: /10

Mood Tracker
Pre-workout: 😊 😅 😐 😜 😣 😎
Post-workout: 😊 😅 😐 😜 😣 😎

Thoughts & Reflections

Did I get enough...
water Y N   sleep Y N

Meals	Today I ate:
• BREAKFAST	
• LUNCH	
• DINNER	
• SNACKS	

TRAINING ENERGY LEVELS
Before   After

Best part about today was ...

Feedback...

Today's Goal:

Powered by
Chlorine
SWIM LOGBOOK

Coach:

Time:

Location:

Date: / /20

S M T W T F S

Pool:
25 ◯ 50 ◯ Other ◯

Weather:

Training Type:
Swim ◯ Dryland ◯ Other ◯

TRAINING SESSION
Nº of laps: .... Distance Swum: ....

WARM-UP MAIN SET COOL-DOWN
INTERVALS SPRINTS DIVES STARTS TURNS
DRILLS PULL BUOY FINS OTHER

Mood Tracker
Pre-workout:
Post-workout:

Thoughts & Reflections

Did I get enough...
water Y N
sleep Y N

Meals	Today I ate:
• BREAKFAST	
• LUNCH	
• DINNER	
• SNACKS	

Total Time Spent In The Water: ....
Rate today's workout: /10

TRAINING ENERGY LEVELS
Before After

Best part about today was ...

Feedback...

Today's Goal:

Powered by
Chlorine
SWIM LOGBOOK

Coach:

Time:

Location:

Date: / /20

S M T W T F S

Pool:
25 ◯ 50 ◯ Other ◯

Training Type:
Swim ◯ Dryland ◯ Other ◯

Weather:

TRAINING SESSION
Nº of laps: .... Distance Swum: ....

WARM-UP MAIN SET COOL-DOWN
INTERVALS SPRINTS DIVES STARTS TURNS
DRILLS PULL BUOY FINS OTHER

Mood Tracker
Pre-workout:
Post-workout:

Thoughts & Reflections

Did I get enough...
water Y N
sleep Y N

Meals	Today I ate:
• BREAKFAST	
• LUNCH	
• DINNER	
• SNACKS	

Total Time Spent In The Water: ....
Rate today's workout: /10

TRAINING ENERGY LEVELS
Before After

Best part about today was ...

Feedback...

Today's Goal:

Powered by
Chlorine
SWIM LOGBOOK

Coach:

Location:

Time:

Date: / /20

S M T W T F S

Training Type:
Swim ◯ Dryland ◯ Other ◯

Pool:
25 ◯ 50 ◯ Other ◯

Weather:

TRAINING SESSION
Nº of laps: .... Distance Swum: ....

WARM-UP MAIN SET COOL-DOWN
INTERVALS SPRINTS DIVES STARTS TURNS
DRILLS PULL BUOY FINS OTHER

Total Time Spent In The Water: ....
Rate today's workout: /10

Mood Tracker
Pre-workout:
Post-workout:

Thoughts & Reflections

Did I get enough...
water   sleep
Y N   Y N

Meals	Today I ate:
• BREAKFAST	
• LUNCH	
• DINNER	
• SNACKS	

TRAINING ENERGY LEVELS
Before   After

Best part about today was ...

Feedback...

Today's Goal:

Powered by
ChloRiNe
SWIM LOGBOOK

Coach:

Location:

Time:

Date: / /20

S M T W T F S

Pool:
25 ○ 50 ○ Other ○

Training Type:
Swim ○ Dryland ○ Other ○

Weather:

TRAINING SESSION
Nº of laps: .... Distance Swum: ....

WARM-UP   MAIN SET   COOL-DOWN
INTERVALS   SPRINTS   DIVES   STARTS   TURNS
DRILLS   PULL BUOY   FINS   OTHER

Mood Tracker
Pre-workout:
Post-workout:

Thoughts & Reflections

Did I get enough...
water   sleep
Y N   Y N

Meals	Today I ate:
• BREAKFAST	
• LUNCH	
• DINNER	
• SNACKS	

Total Time Spent In The Water: ....
Rate today's workout: /10

TRAINING ENERGY LEVELS
Before   After

Best part about today was ...

Feedback...

Today's Goal:

Powered by
Chlorine
SWIM LOGBOOK

Coach:

Location:

Pool: 25 ○ 50 ○ Other ○

Time:

Date: / /20

S M T W T F S

Weather: ☀ ⛅ 🌧 ☔ ❄

Training Type:
Swim ○ Dryland ○ Other ○

TRAINING SESSION
Nº of laps: .... Distance Swum: ....

WARM-UP MAIN SET COOL-DOWN
INTERVALS SPRINTS DIVES STARTS TURNS
DRILLS PULL BUOY FINS OTHER

Total Time Spent In The Water: ....
Rate today's workout: /10

Mood Tracker
Pre-workout: 😊 😨 😐 😠 😣 😎
Post-workout: 😊 😨 😐 😠 😣 😎

Thoughts & Reflections

Did I get enough...
water Y N
sleep Y N

Meals	Today I ate:
• BREAKFAST	
• LUNCH	
• DINNER	
• SNACKS	

TRAINING ENERGY LEVELS
Before After

Best part about today was ...

Feedback...

Today's Goal:

Powered by Chlorine Swim Logbook

Coach:

Time:

Location:

Date: / /20

S M T W T F S

Pool: 25 ◯ 50 ◯ Other ◯

Weather: ☀️ ⛅ 🌦️ 🌧️ ❄️

Training Type: Swim ◯ Dryland ◯ Other ◯

TRAINING SESSION

Nº of laps: .... Distance Swum: ....

WARM-UP MAIN SET COOL-DOWN
INTERVALS SPRINTS DIVES STARTS TURNS
DRILLS PULL BUOY FINS OTHER

Total Time Spent In The Water: ....
Rate today's workout: /10

Mood Tracker
Pre-workout: 🙂 😬 😐 🤪 😠 😡 😎
Post-workout: 🙂 😬 😐 🤪 😠 😡 😎

Thoughts & Reflections

Did I get enough...
water Y N
sleep Y N

Meals	Today I ate:
• BREAKFAST	
• LUNCH	
• DINNER	
• SNACKS	

TRAINING ENERGY LEVELS
Before   After

Best part about today was ...

Feedback...

Today's Goal:

Powered by Chlorine
SWIM LOGBOOK

Coach:

Location:

Time:

Date: / /20

S M T W T F S

Training Type:
Swim ○ Dryland ○ Other ○

Pool:
25 ○ 50 ○ Other ○

Weather:

TRAINING SESSION
Nº of laps: .... Distance Swum: ....

WARM-UP MAIN SET COOL-DOWN
INTERVALS SPRINTS DIVES STARTS TURNS
DRILLS PULL BUOY FINS OTHER

Total Time Spent In The Water: ....
Rate today's workout: /10

Mood Tracker
Pre-workout:
Post-workout:

Thoughts & Reflections

Did I get enough...
water Y N
sleep Y N

Meals	Today I ate:
• BREAKFAST	
• LUNCH	
• DINNER	
• SNACKS	

TRAINING ENERGY LEVELS
Before After

Best part about today was ...

Feedback...

Today's Goal:

Powered by
Chlorine
SWIM LOGBOOK

Coach:

Location:

Pool: 25 ◯ 50 ◯ Other ◯

Time:

Date: /   /20

S M T W T F S

Weather: ☀ ☁ 🌦 🌧 ❄

Training Type:
Swim ◯ Dryland ◯ Other ◯

TRAINING SESSION
Nº of laps: .... Distance Swum: ....

WARM-UP   MAIN SET   COOL-DOWN
INTERVALS   SPRINTS   DIVES   STARTS   TURNS
DRILLS   PULL BUOY   FINS   OTHER

Mood Tracker
Pre-workout: 😊 😀 😐 🙁 😣 😎
Post-workout: 😊 😀 😐 🙁 😣 😎

Thoughts & Reflections
....
....
....
....
....
....

Did I get enough...
water   sleep
Y N   Y N

Meals	Today I ate:
• BREAKFAST	
• LUNCH	
• DINNER	
• SNACKS	

Total Time Spent In The Water: ....
Rate today's workout: /10

TRAINING ENERGY LEVELS
Before   After

Best part about today was ...

Feedback...

Today's Goal:

Powered by
Chlorine
SWIM LOGBOOK

Coach:

Location:

Pool:
25 ○ 50 ○ Other ○

Time:

Date: ___ / ___ /20___

S M T W T F S

Weather:

Training Type:
Swim ○ Dryland ○ Other ○

TRAINING SESSION
Nº of laps: .... Distance Swum: ....

WARM-UP   MAIN SET   COOL-DOWN
INTERVALS SPRINTS DIVES STARTS TURNS
DRILLS PULL BUOY FINS OTHER

Mood Tracker
Pre-workout:
Post-workout:

Thoughts & Reflections

Did I get enough...
water Y N   sleep Y N

Meals	Today I ate:
• BREAKFAST	
• LUNCH	
• DINNER	
• SNACKS	

Total Time Spent In The Water: ....
Rate today's workout: /10

TRAINING ENERGY LEVELS
Before   After

Best part about today was ...

Feedback...

Today's Goal:

Powered by
Chlorine
SWIM LOGBOOK

Coach:

Location:

Pool: 25 ◯ 50 ◯ Other ◯

Training Type:
Swim ◯ Dryland ◯ Other ◯

Time:

Date: ___ / ___ /20___

S M T W T F S

Weather: ☀️ ⛅ 🌧️ ❄️

TRAINING SESSION
Nº of laps: .... Distance Swum: ....

WARM-UP   MAIN SET   COOL-DOWN
INTERVALS SPRINTS DIVES STARTS TURNS
DRILLS   PULL BUOY   FINS   OTHER

Mood Tracker
Pre-workout: 😊 😬 😐 🤪 😠 😎
Post-workout: 😊 😬 😐 🤪 😠 😎

Thoughts & Reflections
_____
_____
_____
_____
_____
_____
_____

Did I get enough...
water Y N   sleep Y N

Meals	Today I ate:
• BREAKFAST	
• LUNCH	
• DINNER	
• SNACKS	

Total Time Spent In The Water: ....
Rate today's workout: /10

TRAINING ENERGY LEVELS
Before   After

Best part about today was ...

Feedback...

Today's Goal:

Powered by
Chlorine
SWIM LOGBOOK

Coach:

Location:

Time:

Date: /   /20

S M T W T F S

Pool: 25◯ 50◯ Other◯

Training Type:
Swim ◯ Dryland ◯ Other ◯

Weather:

TRAINING SESSION
Nº of laps: ....   Distance Swum: ....

WARM-UP   MAIN SET   COOL-DOWN
INTERVALS   SPRINTS   DIVES   STARTS   TURNS
DRILLS   PULL BUOY   FINS   OTHER

Mood Tracker
Pre-workout:
Post-workout:

Thoughts & Reflections

Did I get enough...
water   Y N   sleep   Y N

Meals	Today I ate:
• BREAKFAST	
• LUNCH	
• DINNER	
• SNACKS	

Total Time Spent In The Water: ....
Rate today's workout: /10

TRAINING ENERGY LEVELS
Before   After

Best part about today was ...

Feedback...

Today's Goal:

Powered by
Chlorine
SWIM LOGBOOK

Coach:

Location:

Pool:
25 ○   50 ○   Other ○

Training Type:
Swim ○   Dryland ○   Other ○

Time:

Date: / /20

S M T W T F S

Weather:

TRAINING SESSION
Nº of laps: ....   Distance Swum: ....

WARM-UP   MAIN SET   COOL-DOWN
INTERVALS   SPRINTS   DIVES   STARTS   TURNS
DRILLS   PULL BUOY   FINS   OTHER

Mood Tracker
Pre-workout:
Post-workout:

Thoughts & Reflections

Did I get enough...
water   sleep
Y N   Y N

Meals	Today I ate:
• BREAKFAST	
• LUNCH	
• DINNER	
• SNACKS	

Total Time Spent In The Water: ....
Rate today's workout: /10

TRAINING ENERGY LEVELS
Before   After

Best part about today was ...

Feedback...

Today's Goal:

Powered by
Chlorine
SWIM LOGBOOK

Coach:

Time:

Location:

Date: / /20

S M T W T F S

Pool:
25 ◯ 50 ◯ Other ◯

Weather:
☀ ☁ 🌦 🌧 ❄

Training Type:
Swim ◯ Dryland ◯ Other ◯

TRAINING SESSION
Nº of laps: .... Distance Swum: ....

WARM-UP MAIN SET COOL-DOWN
INTERVALS SPRINTS DIVES STARTS TURNS
DRILLS PULL BUOY FINS OTHER

Mood Tracker
Pre-workout: 😊 😳 😐 😴 😒 😎
Post-workout: 😊 😳 😐 😴 😒 😎

Thoughts & Reflections

Did I get enough...
water Y N   sleep Y N

Meals	Today I ate:
• BREAKFAST	
• LUNCH	
• DINNER	
• SNACKS	

Total Time Spent In The Water: ....
Rate today's workout: /10

TRAINING ENERGY LEVELS
Before — After

Best part about today was ...

Feedback...

Today's Goal:

Powered by
Chlorine
SWIM LOGBOOK

Coach:

Location:

Pool:
25 ◯   50 ◯   Other ◯

Training Type:
Swim ◯   Dryland ◯   Other ◯

Time:

Date: / /20

S M T W T F S

Weather: ☀️ ⛅ 🌦️ ☁️ 🌧️ ❄️

TRAINING SESSION
Nº of laps: ....   Distance Swum: ....

WARM-UP   MAIN SET   COOL-DOWN
INTERVALS   SPRINTS   DIVES   STARTS   TURNS
DRILLS   PULL BUOY   FINS   OTHER

Mood Tracker
Pre-workout: 😀 😳 🙂 🤪 😣 😠 😎
Post-workout: 😀 😳 🙂 🤪 😣 😠 😎

Thoughts & Reflections
_____
_____
_____
_____
_____
_____

Did I get enough...
water   sleep
Y N   Y N

Meals	Today I ate:
• BREAKFAST	
• LUNCH	
• DINNER	
• SNACKS	

Total Time Spent In The Water: ....
Rate today's workout: /10

TRAINING ENERGY LEVELS
Before | After

Best part about today was ...

Feedback...

Today's Goal:

Powered by
Chlorine
SWIM LOGBOOK

Coach:

Location:

Time:

Date: / /20

S M T W T F S

Pool:
25 ◯ 50 ◯ Other ◯

Training Type:
Swim ◯ Dryland ◯ Other ◯

Weather:

TRAINING SESSION
Nº of laps: .... Distance Swum: ....

WARM-UP MAIN SET COOL-DOWN
INTERVALS SPRINTS DIVES STARTS TURNS
DRILLS PULL BUOY FINS OTHER

Mood Tracker
Pre-workout:
Post-workout:

Thoughts & Reflections

Did I get enough...
water   sleep
Y N   Y N

Meals	Today I ate:
• BREAKFAST	
• LUNCH	
• DINNER	
• SNACKS	

Total Time Spent In The Water: ....
Rate today's workout: /10

TRAINING ENERGY LEVELS
Before   After

Best part about today was ...

Feedback...

Today's Goal:

Powered by
Chlorine
SWIM LOGBOOK

Coach:

Time:

Location:

Date: / /20

S M T W T F S

Pool:
25 ◯ 50 ◯ Other ◯

Weather:

Training Type:
Swim ◯ Dryland ◯ Other ◯

TRAINING SESSION
Nº of laps: .... Distance Swum: ....

WARM-UP   MAIN SET   COOL-DOWN
INTERVALS   SPRINTS   DIVES   STARTS   TURNS
DRILLS   PULL BUOY   FINS   OTHER

Mood Tracker
Pre-workout:
Post-workout:

Thoughts & Reflections

Did I get enough...
water   sleep
Y N   Y N

Meals	Today I ate:
• BREAKFAST	
• LUNCH	
• DINNER	
• SNACKS	

Total Time Spent In The Water: ....
Rate today's workout: /10

TRAINING ENERGY LEVELS
Before   After

Best part about today was ...

Feedback...

Today's Goal:

Powered by
Chlorine
SWIM LOGBOOK

Coach:	Time:
Location:	Date: / /20
	S M T W T F S

Training Type:
Swim ◯   Dryland ◯   Other ◯

Pool: 25 ◯   50 ◯   Other ◯

Weather:

TRAINING SESSION
Nº of laps: ....   Distance Swum: ....

WARM-UP   MAIN SET   COOL-DOWN
INTERVALS   SPRINTS   DIVES   STARTS   TURNS
DRILLS   PULL BUOY   FINS   OTHER

Mood Tracker
Pre-workout:
Post-workout:

Thoughts & Reflections

_____
_____
_____
_____
_____

Did I get enough...
water   Y N
sleep   Y N

Meals	Today I ate:
• BREAKFAST	
• LUNCH	
• DINNER	
• SNACKS	

Total Time Spent In The Water: ....
Rate today's workout: /10

TRAINING ENERGY LEVELS
Before   After

Best part about today was ...

Feedback...

Today's Goal:

Powered by
Chlorine
SWIM LOGBOOK

Coach:

Time:

Location:

Date: / /20

S M T W T F S

Training Type:
Swim ○ Dryland ○ Other ○

Pool:
25 ○ 50 ○ Other ○

Weather:

TRAINING SESSION
Nº of laps: .... Distance Swum: ....

WARM-UP MAIN SET COOL-DOWN
INTERVALS SPRINTS DIVES STARTS TURNS
DRILLS PULL BUOY FINS OTHER

Mood Tracker
Pre-workout:
Post-workout:

Thoughts & Reflections

Did I get enough...
water Y N
sleep Y N

Meals	Today I ate:
• BREAKFAST	
• LUNCH	
• DINNER	
• SNACKS	

Total Time Spent In The Water: ....
Rate today's workout: /10

TRAINING ENERGY LEVELS
Before   After

Best part about today was ...

Feedback...

Today's Goal:

Powered by
Chlorine
SWIM LOGBOOK

Coach:

Location:

Pool: 25 ◯ 50 ◯ Other ◯

Time:

Date: / /20

S M T W T F S

Weather:

Training Type:
Swim ◯ Dryland ◯ Other ◯

TRAINING SESSION
Nº of laps: .... Distance Swum: ....

WARM-UP MAIN SET COOL-DOWN
INTERVALS SPRINTS DIVES STARTS TURNS
DRILLS PULL BUOY FINS OTHER

Mood Tracker
Pre-workout:
Post-workout:

Thoughts & Reflections
_____
_____
_____
_____
_____
_____

Did I get enough...
water   sleep
Y N   Y N

Meals	Today I ate:
• BREAKFAST	
• LUNCH	
• DINNER	
• SNACKS	

Total Time Spent In The Water: ....
Rate today's workout: /10

TRAINING ENERGY LEVELS
Before   After

Best part about today was ...

Feedback...

Today's Goal:

Powered by Chlorine
SWIM LOGBOOK

Coach:

Time:

Location:

Date: / /20

S M T W T F S

Pool: 25 ◯ 50 ◯ Other ◯

Weather:

Training Type:
Swim ◯ Dryland ◯ Other ◯

TRAINING SESSION
Nº of laps: .... Distance Swum: ....

WARM-UP   MAIN SET   COOL-DOWN
INTERVALS   SPRINTS   DIVES   STARTS   TURNS
DRILLS   PULL BUOY   FINS   OTHER

Mood Tracker
Pre-workout:
Post-workout:

Thoughts & Reflections

Did I get enough...
water   sleep
Y N   Y N

Meals	Today I ate:
• BREAKFAST	
• LUNCH	
• DINNER	
• SNACKS	

Total Time Spent In The Water: ....
Rate today's workout: /10

TRAINING ENERGY LEVELS
Before   After

Best part about today was ...

Feedback...

Today's Goal:

Powered by
Chlorine
SWIM LOGBOOK

Coach:

Time:

Location:

Date: / /20

S M T W T F S

Pool:
25 ⭕ 50 ⭕ Other ⭕

Weather:

Training Type:
Swim ⭕ Dryland ⭕ Other ⭕

TRAINING SESSION
Nº of laps: .... Distance Swum: ....

WARM-UP   MAIN SET   COOL-DOWN
INTERVALS   SPRINTS   DIVES   STARTS   TURNS
DRILLS   PULL BUOY   FINS   OTHER

Mood Tracker
Pre-workout:
Post-workout:

Thoughts & Reflections

Did I get enough...
water   sleep
Y N   Y N

Meals	Today I ate:
• BREAKFAST	
• LUNCH	
• DINNER	
• SNACKS	

Total Time Spent In The Water: ....
Rate today's workout: /10

TRAINING ENERGY LEVELS
Before   After

Best part about today was ...

Feedback...

Today's Goal:

Powered by
Chlorine
SWIM LOGBOOK

Coach:

Location:

Time:

Date: /   /20

S M T W T F S

Pool:
25 ◯   50 ◯   Other ◯

Weather:

Training Type:
Swim ◯   Dryland ◯   Other ◯

TRAINING SESSION
Nº of laps: ....   Distance Swum: ....

WARM-UP   MAIN SET   COOL-DOWN
INTERVALS   SPRINTS   DIVES   STARTS   TURNS
DRILLS   PULL BUOY   FINS   OTHER

Mood Tracker
Pre-workout:
Post-workout:

Thoughts & Reflections

Did I get enough...
water   sleep
Y N   Y N

Meals	Today I ate:
• BREAKFAST	
• LUNCH	
• DINNER	
• SNACKS	

Total Time Spent In The Water: ....
Rate today's workout: /10

TRAINING ENERGY LEVELS
Before   After

Best part about today was ...

Feedback...

Today's Goal:

Powered by
Chlorine
SWIM LOGBOOK

Coach:

Location:

Pool:
25 ◯ 50 ◯ Other ◯

Time:

Date: / /20

S M T W T F S

Weather: ☀ ☁ 🌦 🌧 ❄

Training Type:
Swim ◯ Dryland ◯ Other ◯

TRAINING SESSION
Nº of laps: .... Distance Swum: ....

WARM-UP MAIN SET COOL-DOWN
INTERVALS SPRINTS DIVES STARTS TURNS
DRILLS PULL BUOY FINS OTHER

Mood Tracker
Pre-workout: 😊 😳 😐 🤪 😣 😎
Post-workout: 😊 😳 😐 🤪 😣 😎

Thoughts & Reflections

....
....
....
....
....
....

Did I get enough...
water   sleep
Y N   Y N

Meals	Today I ate:
• BREAKFAST	
• LUNCH	
• DINNER	
• SNACKS	

Total Time Spent In The Water: ....
Rate today's workout: /10

TRAINING ENERGY LEVELS
Before   After

Best part about today was ...

Feedback...

Today's Goal:

Powered by
Chlorine
SWIM LOGBOOK

Coach:

Location:

Pool:
25 ○ 50 ○ Other ○

Time:

Date: / /20

S M T W T F S

Training Type:
Swim ○ Dryland ○ Other ○

Weather: ☀️ ⛅ 🌦️ ☁️ ❄️

TRAINING SESSION
Nº of laps: .... Distance Swum: ....

WARM-UP MAIN SET COOL-DOWN
INTERVALS SPRINTS DIVES STARTS TURNS
DRILLS PULL BUOY FINS OTHER

Total Time Spent In The Water: ....
Rate today's workout: /10

Mood Tracker
Pre-workout: 😊 😄 😐 😖 😠 😎
Post-workout: 😊 😄 😐 😖 😠 😎

Thoughts & Reflections

Did I get enough...
water   sleep
Y N   Y N

Meals	Today I ate:
• BREAKFAST	
• LUNCH	
• DINNER	
• SNACKS	

TRAINING ENERGY LEVELS
Before | After

Best part about today was ...

Feedback...

Today's Goal:

Powered by
Chlorine
SWIM LOGBOOK

Coach:

Location:

Pool:
25 ◯ 50 ◯ Other ◯

Training Type:
Swim ◯ Dryland ◯ Other ◯

Time:

Date: / /20

S M T W T F S

Weather: ☀ ☁ 🌦 🌧 ❄

TRAINING SESSION
Nº of laps: .... Distance Swum: ....

WARM-UP   MAIN SET   COOL-DOWN
INTERVALS SPRINTS DIVES STARTS TURNS
DRILLS PULL BUOY FINS OTHER

Mood Tracker
Pre-workout: 😊 😟 😐 😣 😠 😎
Post-workout: 😊 😟 😐 😣 😠 😎

Thoughts & Reflections

....
....
....
....
....
....

Did I get enough...
water   sleep
Y N   Y N

Meals	Today I ate:
• BREAKFAST	
• LUNCH	
• DINNER	
• SNACKS	

Total Time Spent In The Water: ....
Rate today's workout: /10

TRAINING ENERGY LEVELS
Before   After

Best part about today was ...

Feedback...

Today's Goal:

Powered by
Chlorine
SWIM LOGBOOK

Coach:

Time:

Location:

Date: / /20

S M T W T F S

Pool:
25 ○ 50 ○ Other ○

Weather:

Training Type:
Swim ○ Dryland ○ Other ○

TRAINING SESSION
Nº of laps: .... Distance Swum: ....

WARM-UP   MAIN SET   COOL-DOWN
INTERVALS   SPRINTS   DIVES   STARTS   TURNS
DRILLS   PULL BUOY   FINS   OTHER

Mood Tracker
Pre-workout:
Post-workout:

Thoughts & Reflections

Did I get enough...
water   sleep
Y N   Y N

Meals	Today I ate:
• BREAKFAST	
• LUNCH	
• DINNER	
• SNACKS	

Total Time Spent In The Water: ....
Rate today's workout: /10

TRAINING ENERGY LEVELS
Before   After

Best part about today was ...

Feedback...

Today's Goal:

Powered by
Chlorine
SWIM LOGBOOK

Coach:

Location:

Time:

Date: /   /20

S   M   T   W   T   F   S

Pool:
25 ◯   50 ◯   Other ◯

Training Type:
Swim ◯   Dryland ◯   Other ◯

Weather:

TRAINING SESSION
Nº of laps: ....   Distance Swum: ....

WARM-UP   MAIN SET   COOL-DOWN
INTERVALS   SPRINTS   DIVES   STARTS   TURNS
DRILLS   PULL BUOY   FINS   OTHER

Mood Tracker
Pre-workout:
Post-workout:

Thoughts & Reflections

Did I get enough...
water   sleep
Y N   Y N

Meals	Today I ate:
• BREAKFAST	
• LUNCH	
• DINNER	
• SNACKS	

Total Time Spent In The Water: ....
Rate today's workout: /10

TRAINING ENERGY LEVELS
Before   After

Best part about today was ...

Feedback...

Today's Goal:

Powered by
Chlorine
SWIM LOGBOOK

Coach:

Location:

Pool:
25 ◯ 50 ◯ Other ◯

Time:

Date: /   /20

S M T W T F S

Weather: ☀️ ⛅ 🌥️ 🌧️ ❄️

Training Type:
Swim ◯ Dryland ◯ Other ◯

TRAINING SESSION
Nº of laps: .... Distance Swum: ....

WARM-UP MAIN SET COOL-DOWN
INTERVALS SPRINTS DIVES STARTS TURNS
DRILLS PULL BUOY FINS OTHER

Mood Tracker
Pre-workout: 😊 😬 😐 🥴 😠 😎
Post-workout: 😊 😬 😐 🥴 😠 😎

Thoughts & Reflections

Did I get enough...
water   sleep
Y N   Y N

Meals	Today I ate:
• BREAKFAST	
• LUNCH	
• DINNER	
• SNACKS	

Total Time Spent In The Water: ....
Rate today's workout: /10

TRAINING ENERGY LEVELS
Before   After

Best part about today was ...

Feedback...

Today's Goal:

Powered by
Chlorine
SWIM **LOGBOOK**

Coach:

Location:

Pool:
25 ◯ 50 ◯ Other ◯

Training Type:
Swim ◯ Dryland ◯ Other ◯

Time:

Date: / /20

S M T W T F S

Weather:
☀ ⛅ 🌦 🌧 ❄

TRAINING SESSION
Nº of laps: .... Distance Swum: ....

WARM-UP MAIN SET COOL-DOWN
INTERVALS SPRINTS DIVES STARTS TURNS
DRILLS PULL BUOY FINS OTHER

Total Time Spent In The Water: ....
Rate today's workout: /10

Mood Tracker
Pre-workout: 😊 😴 😐 😣 😠 😎
Post-workout: 😊 😴 😐 😣 😠 😎

Thoughts & Reflections
....
....
....
....
....

Did I get enough...
water Y N   sleep Y N

Meals	Today I ate:
• BREAKFAST	
• LUNCH	
• DINNER	
• SNACKS	

TRAINING ENERGY LEVELS
Before   After

Best part about today was ...

Feedback...

Today's Goal:

Powered by
Chlorine
SWIM LOGBOOK

Coach:

Time:

Location:

Date: / /20

S M T W T F S

Pool:
25 ◯ 50 ◯ Other ◯

Weather:

Training Type:
Swim ◯ Dryland ◯ Other ◯

TRAINING SESSION
Nº of laps: .... Distance Swum: ....

WARM-UP MAIN SET COOL-DOWN
INTERVALS SPRINTS DIVES STARTS TURNS
DRILLS PULL BUOY FINS OTHER

Mood Tracker
Pre-workout: 😅 🙂 😵 😣 😠 😎
Post-workout: 🙂 😅 😣 😠 😫 😎

Thoughts & Reflections

Did I get enough...
water   sleep
Y N   Y N

Meals	Today I ate:
• BREAKFAST	
• LUNCH	
• DINNER	
• SNACKS	

Total Time Spent In The Water: ....
Rate today's workout: /10

TRAINING ENERGY LEVELS
Before   After

Best part about today was ...

Feedback...

Today's Goal:

Powered by
Chlorine
SWIM LOGBOOK

Coach:

Location:

Pool: 25 ◯ 50 ◯ Other ◯

Training Type:
Swim ◯ Dryland ◯ Other ◯

Time:

Date: ___ / ___ /20___

S M T W T F S

Weather: ☀️ ⛅ 🌦️ 🌧️ ❄️

TRAINING SESSION
Nº of laps: .... Distance Swum: ....

WARM-UP   MAIN SET   COOL-DOWN
INTERVALS SPRINTS DIVES STARTS TURNS
DRILLS PULL BUOY FINS OTHER

Total Time Spent In The Water: ....
Rate today's workout: /10

Mood Tracker
Pre-workout: 😊 😅 😐 😣 😠 😎
Post-workout: 😊 😅 😐 😣 😠 😎

Thoughts & Reflections
_____
_____
_____
_____
_____
_____

Did I get enough...
water   sleep
Y N   Y N

Meals	Today I ate:
• BREAKFAST	
• LUNCH	
• DINNER	
• SNACKS	

TRAINING ENERGY LEVELS
Before   After

Best part about today was ...

Feedback...

Today's Goal:

Powered by
Chlorine
SWIM **LOGBOOK**

Coach:

Time:

Location:

Date: / /20

S M T W T F S

Pool:
25 ◯ 50 ◯ Other ◯

Weather:

Training Type:
Swim ◯ Dryland ◯ Other ◯

TRAINING SESSION
Nº of laps: .... Distance Swum: ....

WARM-UP   MAIN SET   COOL-DOWN
INTERVALS   SPRINTS   DIVES   STARTS   TURNS
DRILLS   PULL BUOY   FINS   OTHER

Total Time Spent In The Water: ....
Rate today's workout: /10

Mood Tracker
Pre-workout:
Post-workout:

Thoughts & Reflections

Did I get enough...
water   sleep
Y N   Y N

Meals	Today I ate:
• BREAKFAST	
• LUNCH	
• DINNER	
• SNACKS	

TRAINING ENERGY LEVELS
Before   After

Best part about today was …

Feedback...

Today's Goal:

Powered by
Chlorine
SWIM LOGBOOK

Coach:

Location:

Pool:
25 ○ 50 ○ Other ○

Time:

Date: / /20

S M T W T F S

Training Type:
Swim ○ Dryland ○ Other ○

Weather:

TRAINING SESSION
Nº of laps: .... Distance Swum: ....

WARM-UP   MAIN SET   COOL-DOWN
INTERVALS SPRINTS DIVES STARTS TURNS
DRILLS   PULL BUOY   FINS   OTHER

Mood Tracker
Pre-workout:
Post-workout:

Thoughts & Reflections
....
....
....
....
....
....
....

Did I get enough...
water   sleep
Y N   Y N

Meals	Today I ate:
• BREAKFAST	
• LUNCH	
• DINNER	
• SNACKS	

Total Time Spent In The Water: ....
Rate today's workout: /10

TRAINING ENERGY LEVELS
Before   After

Best part about today was ...

Feedback...

Today's Goal:

Powered by Chlorine
PB TRACKER

Date	Pool Type	Location	Stroke	Distance	PB Time	External Factors	Internal Factors

Powered by Chlorine PB Tracker

Date	Pool Type	Location	Stroke	Distance	PB Time	External Factors	Internal Factors